SYRIE-PALESTINE
SYRIEN-PALÄSTINA
SIRIA-PALESTINA
SYRIA-PALESTINE

JAPAN	Vadime Elisseeff, Curator at the Cernuschi Museum, Paris
MESOPOTAMIA	Jean-Claude Margueron, Member of the French Institute of Archaeology, Beirut
MEXICO	Jacques Soustelle
PERSIA I (From the origins to the Achaemenids)	Jean-Louis Huot, Member of the French Institute of Archaeology, Beirut
PERSIA II (From the Seleucids to the Sassanids)	Vladimir G. Lukonin, Head of the Oriental Department, Hermitage Museum, Leningrad
PERU	† Rafael Larco Hoyle, Director of the Rafael Larco Herrera Museum, Lima
PREHISTORY	Denise de Sonneville-Bordes, Ph. D.
ROMANIA	Constantin Daicoviciu, Director of the Archaeological Institute of Cluj, and Emil Condurachi, Director of the Archaeological Institute of Bucarest
ROME	Gilbert Picard, Professor at the University of Paris-Sorbonne
SOUTHERN CAUCASUS	Boris B. Piotrovsky, Director of the Hermitage Museum, Leningrad
SOUTHERN SIBERIA	Mikhail Gryaznov, Professor at the Archaeological Institute, Leningrad
SYRIA-PALESTINE I (Prehistory and Ancient Orient)	Jean Perrot, Head of the French Archaeological Mission in Israel
THAILAND	Pisit Charoenwongsa and C. Subhadradis Diskul, Professor at the Silpakorn University, Bankok
TRANSHIMALAYA	Giuseppe Tucci, President of the Italian Institute for the Middle and Far East, Rome
URARTU	Boris B. Piotrovsky, Director of the Hermitage Museum, Leningrad

ARCHAEOLOGIA MVNDI

Series prepared under the direction of Jean Marcadé, Professor of Archaeology at the University of Bordeaux

AHARON KEMPINSKI
MICHAEL AVI-YONAH

SYRIA-PALESTINE II

FROM THE MIDDLE BRONZE AGE
TO THE END OF THE CLASSICAL WORLD (2200 B.C. - 324 A.D.)

21 illustrations in colour,
64 in black and white

NAGEL PUBLISHERS, GENEVA - PARIS - MUNICH

ISBN 2-8263-0694-4

CONTENTS

EDITOR'S NOTE

This volume of the Archaeologia Mundi *series is a double one. The first part, by Dr. Aharon Kempinski, covers the two millennia between the early period surveyed in* Syria-Palestine I *and the classical period which is the subject of the second part, written by the late Professor Avi-Yonah (whose untimely death prevented him from seeing his work through the press).* Archaeologia Mundi *thus offers its readers a complete survey of Syro-Palestinian archaeology from the earliest times to the end of the ancient world.*

Set against this advantage, the possible objection to including two studies by different authors within the same volume seemed of little weight. It has, after all, long been the practice in the publication of scientific works to have different chapters written by experts in particular subjects. If the reader of this volume observes certain differences in tone and presentation between the two parts this is no more than a reflection of individual personalities and temperaments ; and these differences are themselves instructive.

The separate bibliographies for the two parts have been brought together at the end of the volume. There is inevitably some degree of overlap between the two, but this seems a small price to pay for the convenience of having the references arranged according to subject-matter ; and this layout will also of course facilitate the reading of the main text.

J.M.

Acknowledgments

We should like to express our gratitude to the following persons and institutions : Mr. G. Barakat, Ministry of Tourism and Antiquities, Hashemite Kingdom of Jordan ; Mr. Sami Rababy, Beirut ; Mrs. H. Katzenstein, Israel Department of Antiquities and Museums ; Mrs. I. Pommerantz, Israel Department of Antiquities and Museums ; Mrs. I. Levitt, Israel Museum ; Rabbi S. Nathan, Director, Ministry of Tourism, Jerusalem. The Beirut Museum, Damascus Museum, Antakya Museum, Ny Carlsberg Glyptotek, Copenhagen, Israel Exploration Society, Tell Mardikh Expedition (Rome University) and Tel Aviv University also assisted by providing photographs, and for this we are likewise grateful.

PREFACE

The pattern of archaeological research does not differ only from province to province of its vast domain : even within a single region it may have very different aspects. Thus Syro-Palestinian archaeology, which for the earliest periods employs the methods of prehistoric research and is to some extent concerned with problems common to the whole of the ancient East, changes in character when it comes to the so-called " classical" period. The written sources are now abundant and explicit ; the material remains are substantial, often covering considerable areas ; and the imprint of Hellenistic and Greco-Roman civilisation is readily recognisable. The questions which now arise are not so much historical and chronological as cultural, artistic and religious problems.

The main facts being thus established, the archaeologist is chiefly concerned with why *things happened and* how *they happened ; with tracing events back to their earliest beginnings, identifying and precisely defining particular influences, and following in detail the changes which can be observed. For this purpose comparative studies become of prime importance, equally with stratigraphic study. Excavation methods can perhaps afford to be less meticulous when the excavator is dealing with remains of such considerable extent as some of the sites of this period ; but against this a high degree of accuracy in reconstruction and restoration, an exact understanding of architectural structures and a thorough stylistic analysis of figured material are necessary to distinguish the adaptations and borrowings, the long-term trends and the passing fashions, the genuinely original variants and the mere provincial fumblings.*

In the last analysis the most significant results of archaeological investigation in this territory may lie not in the enlargement of our knowledge of the glamorous and spectacular sites like Baalbek and Palmyra, Dura and Petra, but in less obvious directions. In these regions the encounter between Greece and the ancient East, the ferment of Judaism and the magnificence of the Roman Empire stimulated a renewal of the classical

13

tradition in varied forms. Certain particular types of building, certain iconographic types and certain aesthetic principles developed in Syria and Palestine were carried in the train of the legions and found their way into western Europe. It must be of concern to us to study the genesis of these features.

J.M.

Part I

*From the Middle Bronze Age
to the Classical Period (2200 B.C. - 332 B.C.)*

Aharon Kempinski

Translated from the Hebrew by R. Grafman

INTRODUCTION

THE GEOGRAPHICAL BACKGROUND (by M. Avi-Yonah)

Syria and Palestine together form the western arc of the so-called " Fertile Crescent ", the belt of cultivable land encircling the Arabian desert on its northern side. Both countries are shaped by two parallel mountain ridges, running from north to south. The western ridge, consisting of the Lebanese mountains and their continuations in Galilee, Judaea and Samaria, follows the Mediterranean coast. The distance between the mountains and the sea varies : in the north they come quite close to the coast, while to the south they leave a gradually widening plain. The mountain chain is broken by occasional gaps (the Massyaf gap, the Esdraelon valley) which connect the coast with the interior. A series of river valleys formed by the Orontes, the Leontes and the Jordan pass between the two mountain chains, with an ample supply of water and a fertile soil which favour settlement. The eastern mountain ridge, formed by Mount Hermon and the hills of Gilead, Moab and Edom, borders the desert, beyond which lie the Euphrates and Tigris valleys. This ridge is fertile on its western slopes ; the width of the cultivable area on its eastern side varies from north to south.

Geography thus favoured urban development along the coast, in the river valleys and to some extent in the transverse valleys and the eastern mountains. Beyond this a few oases (Palmyra, Damascus) made possible more concentrated settlement. The narrowness of the Syrian coastal strip forced the Phoenician cities from early times into seafaring in order to compensate for their lack of arable land.

Comparing Syria with Palestine, we notice the generally wider extent of the natural features in the north. At the 36th parallel the Euphrates bend comes within 200 kilometres of the Mediterranean, creating a potentially cultivable area in the Antioch-Thapsacus-Hama triangle. Farther south this area is reduced in width until it runs into the Negeb wilderness and the Sinai desert. Rainfall is also more abundant in the north, both in quantity and in terms of the area covered.

1

2

3

4

5

9

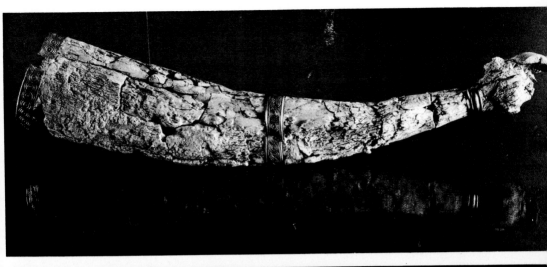

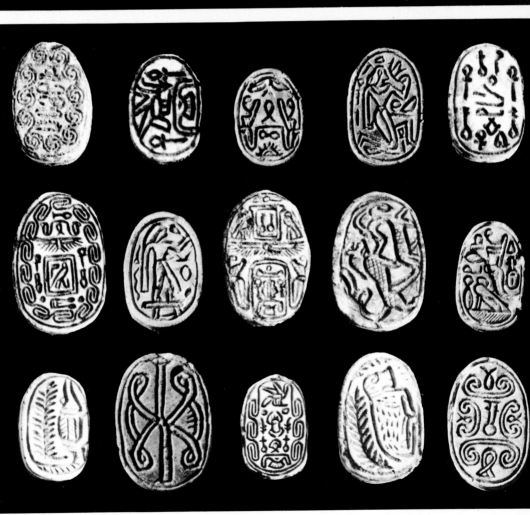

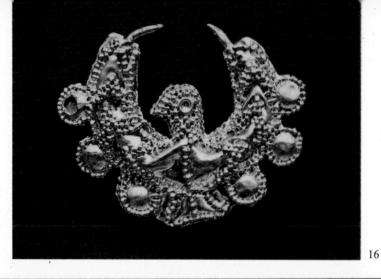

16   17

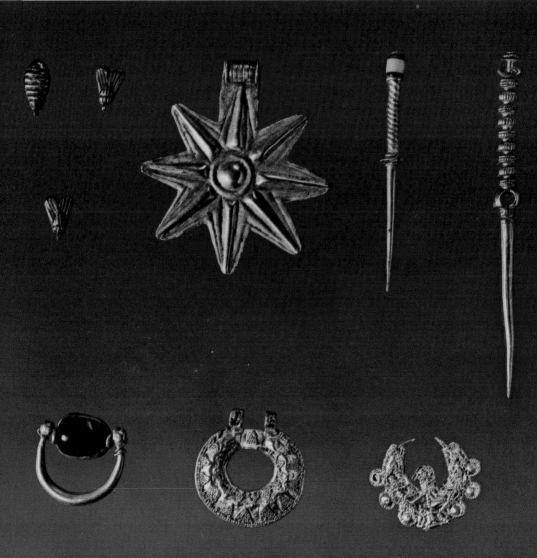

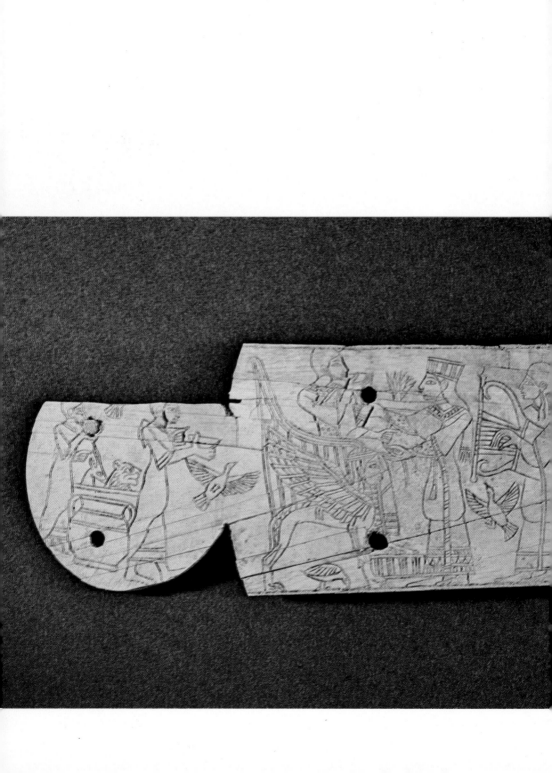

19

20

21

To sum up, therefore, conditions of life in the north (Syria) are on the whole more favourable for the rise of civilisation in its material aspects, the struggle between " the desert and the sown " less bitter ; while in the south (Palestine) life is harsher and the contrasts more absolute.

ARCHAEOLOGY IN THE 19th CENTURY (to the End of the First World War)

The foundations of modern archaeological and historical research in Syria and Palestine were laid during the first half of the 19th century. The travels of Edward Robinson in Palestine and parts of Syria and Lebanon from 1838 onwards led to the identification of many sites and mounds with places mentioned in the Biblical sources. Only in the last third of the century, however, was proper mapping and surveying of the various sites initiated. In 1871-77 the Palestine Exploration Fund compiled a record of the known sites, with accompanying maps, under the direction of Conder and Kitchener. At the same time de Saulcy and Warren began their activities in Jerusalem. Indeed the 19th century was the period of blossoming of Palestinology. In contrast, and in spite of its even greater historical importance, Syria was neglected. This situation was aggravated by the added incentive which the Bible gave to Palestinian archaeology from its very inception — still a important factor today. Interest in Syria came early in the 20th century, with the advance of archaeological and historical research in the adjacent lands of Mesopotamia and Anatolia. The first mound to be the subject of proper scientific investigation was Tell el-Hesi in southern Palestine, excavated by Flinders Petrie in 1890. It was here for the first time that Petrie distinguished the different strata and realised the importance of pottery for dating them. He also identified Palestinian vessels which had been imported into Egypt in ancient times and were found on Egyptian sites along with Egyptian objects which were readily datable ; they thus provided a means of dating similar vessels in the various strata at Tell el-Hesi, and hence of dating the strata themselves. This method is still valid today and is currently used for determining chronology in all scientific excavations in Syria and Palestine.

In the early part of the present century, before the first world war, a number of large excavations were conducted on Biblical sites in Palestine and Syria — at Gezer by Macalister, at Jericho by Sellin and Watzinger, at Megiddo by Schumacher. In these excavations the first steps were taken towards the correct assignment of finds to specific strata: in comparison with Petrie's work at Tell el-Hesi, however, these later scholars were still using primitive methods. During the same period the first large-scale excavations in northern Syria were taking place at Carchemish, directed by D.G. Hogarth on behalf of the British Museum (1908-11). But the fine stratigraphic work done by Humann and Koldewey at Zincirli, on the Syro-Anatolian border, and the architectural and stratigraphic investigation by Dörpfeld at Troy were on a much higher scientific level. Clearly Syro-Palestinian archaeology was still far behind other neighbouring countries at the beginning of this century.

RESEARCH BETWEEN THE WARS

After the first world war, when Syria and Palestine came under French and British mandate, archaeological research in these countries was brought fully within the framework of European archaeology. In Syria the first large French excavations were carried out at Byblos, Qatna, Hama and Ugarit. In Palestine excavations at Tell Beit Mirsim from 1926 onwards enabled Albright to establish a stratigraphic series for most of the Bronze and Iron Ages ; indeed this site became a landmark for all subsequent work in Palestinian and Syrian archaeology.

Between 1925 and 1939 excavations at the city of Megiddo confirmed the pattern revealed at Tell Beit Mirsim and added an important sequence for the Early Bronze Age, which was altogether lacking at Tell Beit Mirsim. The impressive stratigraphic work at Megiddo also revealed significant links between Syria, Palestine and the Phoenician coast. In the late thirties two important scientific projects were carried out in northern Syria. The first was the excavation of a number of mounds in the Amuq region as part of a regional project — a method repeated only quite recently in the Syro-Palestinian region. The second was the impressive work done by Sir Leonard Woolley at Alalakh, where, using methods developed in Mesopotamia, he excavated the citadel area of the city, which served throughout the 2nd millennium B.C. as capital of the land of Mukiš (the modern Amuq). Using these methods, which were based on accurate stratigraphy, Woolley discovered two archives of different periods, making Alalakh a key point in unravelling the chronology of the whole of northern Syria, and hence also of Palestine.

PROGRESS SINCE THE SECOND WORLD WAR

In the 1950s and 1960s a number of foreign expeditions continued working in Syria, particularly at Byblos, Ugarit, Tell Sukas and Tell Mardikh, and in the early seventies a regional project was launched near Meskene, in an area due to be flooded on completion of the Euphrates dam. The activities of the Syrian Department of Antiquities included a number of notable rescue excavations at various sites throughout the country, including the Neo-Hittite site of Tell Dara.

Several foreign expeditions also continued to work in Palestine during this period. At Jericho Miss Kenyon extended Garstang's trenches and developed a new stratigraphic method. At Shechem Wright carried on the work begun by the German excavations of the thirties and sought to redefine the stratigraphy proposed by the earlier excavators. In the early sixties Miss Kenyon transferred her activities to Jerusalem, achieving impressive results.

The activities of Israeli archaeologists began, for all practical purposes, with the excavations at Hazor, under the direction of Yadin, Aharoni, Ruth

Amiran, Dunayevsky, M. and Trude Dothan, and Perrot. It was here that the "Israeli" stratigraphic method was first developed, later to be refined at other sites. Tel Dan, excavated in recent years, has become of great importance for the understanding of the connections between Palestine and central and northern Syria. At Ashdod, Ramat Rahel, Arad, Beersheba and Lachish recent work has revealed several Iron Age strata, greatly advancing archaeological knowledge of the period of the Bible.

METHODS OF RESEARCH

In contrast to their near neighbours, Syria and Palestine are poor in written documents ; in Syria two archives have been found, at Alalakh and Ugarit, while in Palestine a meagre archive came to light at Taanach. In both countries numbers of clay tablets with inscriptions in cuneiform script have been found at various sites. The inscribed Egyptian finds are only rarely of assistance in dating the strata in which they were found. In the Iron Age, with the spread of an alphabetic script, the use of writing became commoner than in the Bronze Age ; but most documents were written on perishable materials, and only a few on potsherds or stone. Northern Syria is exceptional in yielding numerous inscriptions on stelae or statues of the Neo-Hittite period.

In consequence greater emphasis must be placed on small finds for dating the architectural remains in the various strata. The observation and recording of the relationship between finds and their context, and their stratigraphic association with structures, is the very core of archaeological fieldwork. In the excavations carried out in the earlier part of this century this principle was not closely adhered to, and only recently has it been rigorously applied. Indeed there are now two schools of thought among excavators in the Syro-Palestinian region. One, the "section school", which has crystallised in recent years round Miss Kenyon and her disciples, pays maximum attention to sections and baulks, and thus prefers excavating in narrow trenches, with both faces providing sections, or in square excavations widely separated by large baulks ; in both cases the sections provide the principal guide in fieldwork. The other school, which might be called the " architectural school ", is the traditional method evolved in the Middle East over the last hundred years, and involves opening up the maximum possible area so that architectural complexes can be excavated as units. This method can provide a clearer understanding of the excavation as a whole ; and with the exposure of comprehensible architectural complexes and the identification of the various floor levels within them (including the related finds) it is possible to obtain fairly precise dating.

The Kenyon method emphasises the importance of the pottery found within and beneath the floors of the structures, which provides a *post quem* date for the architectural units (in so far as these have been defined). The architectural method regards the pottery found *on* the floors, and the size of the assemblages (if sufficient in quantity to ensure correct dating) as the major means of dating, generally providing *ante quem* dates for the structures. The existence of these two different approaches to excavation has of course led to the development of further variations, and each archaeologist strives to achieve a method of excavation suited to his particular site — or often, unfortunately, suited to the financial resources at his disposal.

THE MIDDLE BRONZE AGE

I

1. MIDDLE BRONZE AGE I

The Historical Framework

As in the Early Bronze Age, control of Syria and Palestine during this period oscillated between the major political powers, the kingdom of Egypt to the south and the large Mesopotamian kingdoms to the north-east. But in contrast with the position in the 3rd millennium the historical documentation at the beginning of the 2nd millennium is considerable, making it possible to establish the various political associations and relationships within this region.

In the final century and a half of the 3rd millennium the splendid urban culture of the Early Bronze Age degenerated and was then destroyed, largely as a result of the blocking of the trade routes between the extremities of the Fertile Crescent by nomads. The decline of Egypt during the Sixth Dynasty, and of Mesopotamia and northern Syria under the Akkadian empire, were also contributory factors. With the destruction of the economic basis of this urban culture there was a gradual increase in nomadic penetration into the settled areas, until by the beginning of the 21st century B.C. most of Palestine and southern Syria had come under the control of nomadic or semi-nomadic tribes. The period during which this nomadic rule was established is known as Middle Bronze Age I or, in Miss Kenyon's terminology, the Intermediate Early Bronze-Middle Bronze period. (In the following discussion the traditional or American terminology is used).

Cultural Dualism in Syria and Phoenicia

This nomadic penetration did not occur throughout Syria, and certainly not along the whole Phoenician coast. In the middle and lower Orontes region of northern Syria and in a number of enclaves on the Phoenician coast the Early Bronze Age culture continued to develop, though occasionally influenced by features of the nomadic culture. In northern Syria, along the lower Orontes, a well developed urban culture flourished. An outstanding example of this culture is provided by Alalakh strata XIV-XII ; here Syrian painted pottery first appears — a feature which became one of the characteristics of the succeeding cultural phase. A similar process can be detected at the coastal city of Byblos, where the Early Bronze Age culture developed directly into the Middle Bronze IIA phase, with no intervening Middle Bronze I. This situation — of two cultures existing side by side — is clearly reflected in the mounds of the Amuq plain and at Ugarit, where elements of the Hama stratum J (Middle Bronze Age I) culture appear along with local elements *(Plate 15)*. Hama (the Biblical Hamath), on the middle Orontes, reveals in stratum J, which is composed of several sub-strata, a permanent settlement which was apparently a regional centre for the nomadic tribes. The Hama culture spread along the upper Orontes into the northern parts of Palestine. This culture is characterised mainly by delicate wheel-made pottery (goblets and " teapots "). The fabric is black or grey, with decoration in white or pale yellow *(Plates 4, 5)*.

The Nomadic Culture in Palestine

Two principal pottery types can be identified in Palestine during this period, each apparently associated with a major nomadic group. The northern type is connected with pottery imports and direct influence from Hama, as well as from the remnants of the Early Bronze Age culture which still survived on the Phoenician coast. It is associated with a rich metal industry, which has clear links with northern Syria and Anatolia. The culture of this northern group belongs to a nomadic people, the Amorites, whose ties with the Orontes region are known from the later documents of the Mari period (19th-18th centuries B.C.). The southern group is more homogeneous and has few connections with the northern group ; the " teapots " *(Plate 3)* are a local imitation of a type common in the Hama culture. Local elements dating from the end of Early Bronze Age IIIB are quite apparent here, as are this group's genetic links with Transjordan. It would seem that these nomads penetrated westward across the Jordan during the period of decline and collapse of the Early Bronze Age culture. This population, which was apparently Semitic, set up temporary settlements in the central Negeb, in parts of the Sinai peninsula, in the Judaean hills and in the southern coastal plain of Palestine. An interesting example of a temporary settlement of this kind was excavated near Sede-Boker in the central Negeb; its character indicates that the population consisted of shepherds who also practised metal-working.

The nomadic character of the Middle Bronze Age I inhabitants is reflected also in their cemeteries, which are found throughout Palestine and parts of southern Syria and are indicative of the forms of ancestor worship then practised. There are several types of burial, two of which are notable: (a) tombs with deep shafts (up to 5 metres) and a small burial chamber, generally containing a single burial, in which the dead man was accompanied by pottery or his personal weapons; and (b) tumuli, in which the dead man was buried in a cist, the cist then being covered over and a tumulus erected over the burial. In Transjordan burial was usually in a dolmen, which was also covered by a tumulus. The latter form of burial appears to have originated in the nomadic cultures of Transjordan and Syria; the oldest examples date from the last phase of the Early Bronze Age.

2. MIDDLE BRONZE AGE II

New Imperial Interests

Towards the end of the 21st century B.C., during the phase known as Middle Bronze Age IIA, two developments brought about radical changes in the political and cultural situation in Syria and Palestine. The northern and central parts of Syria were annexed by the rulers of the Third Dynasty at Ur. There is evidence of this at Byblos on the Phoenician coast, where the local governor, Ibdadi, was "appointed" by Ur; and a fragment of a Sumerian lexical list was found on the same site. Of approximately the same date, but associated with Middle Bronze Age I pottery, is a silver goblet from Ein Samiya near Ramallah in central Palestine; this bears a mythological scene in the North Syrian style, which was influenced during this period by the Sumero-Akkadian culture of Mesopotamia *(Plates 1, 2)*. The control of parts of Syria by Ur led to increasing urbanisation in northern and central Syria, and it was during this period that the large cities like Tell Mardikh in northern Syria flourished. At this site were found art objects belonging to the period of the Third Dynasty at Ur *(Plates 6, 8)*, as well as an Akkadian inscription on a statue identifying the site as the city of Ebla, which had been one of the most important centres in Syria during the 3rd millennium.

The Egyptians in Palestine

In the south, in the Palestinian coastal plain and later along the Phoenician-Syrian coast, Egyptian influence spread during the late Eleventh and Twelfth Dynasties, beginning in the 20th century B.C. This influence was felt first at those urban centres which had not submitted to the Middle Bronze Age I nomads, and it was here that the new culture of Middle Bronze Age IIA began to emerge.

This initial period of Egyptian rule over parts of Palestine finds expression in a particular type of Egyptian document — the Execration Texts, which provide formulae for cursing potential rebel vassals of the king of Egypt. Two principal groups of such texts are known, one dating from the beginning of Twelfth Dynasty rule in Palestine and on the Phoenician coast (early 20th century ?), the other from a later stage of the same dynasty or possibly the beginning of the Thirteenth Dynasty. The earlier group gives us

41

the names of rulers and settlements in Palestine and along the Phoenician coast, and it is here that we find the earliest mention of many of the important cities later known from the Bible, like Ashkelon, Jerusalem and Rehob; while along the coast appear Gebal (Byblos), Arqa and Ullaza. In most cases the names of several rulers are given for a single settlement, which would point to a tribal form of rule. Egyptian influence is demonstrated most clearly at the port town of Byblos, where a number of temples have been excavated containing a wealth of Egyptian objects from the beginning of the Middle Kingdom. As already noted, the settlement at Byblos passed directly from the end of Early Bronze Age III to the beginning of Middle Bronze Age IIA. In Palestine there is a close analogy to this continuity in the stratigraphic sequence of the cultic structures at Megiddo, where one of the Early Bronze Age temples continued into Middle Bronze Age I, forming a core round which the sacred area developed at the beginning of Middle Bronze Age IIA.

Settlement of the Interior

In the mid 20th century there was a large-scale renewal of settlement in Palestine and southern Syria. Many sites were now reoccupied, and numerous entirely new settlements were founded. In southern Palestine a large town was established at Tell el-Ajjul (Sharuhen?), and urban settlement was renewed at Tell Beit Mirsim and Lachish. In central Palestine Shechem was founded and Aphek, at the source of the river Yarkon, was resettled. In northern Palestine the settlement at Megiddo was reorganised and fortified, and in the Akko plain cities were founded at Tell Kisan, Tell Kabri and later at Akko itself. In the upper Jordan valley settlement was renewed at Laish (Tel Dan) and Hazor.

This trend was influenced by two factors. The first stemmed from the cities on the coast, whose colonising activities carried with them such cultural elements as building traditions which still partly dated from the Early

Bronze Age as well as specific types of pottery. Among the latter were types with a dark red burnish and forms imitating metal-ware ; and there were also pottery forms which clearly continued Early Bronze Age III types. The other factor was immigration along the great Syro-African rift (the Orontes-Biqa-Jordan valleys) of elements from northern Syria, particularly from the Khabur and lower Orontes valleys. These peoples brought with them the painted pottery typical of these regions, and thus introduced this pottery — with red and black decoration on a light ground — into northern Palestine *(Plate 7)*. This ware was typical of the northern part of the country during the entire Middle Bronze Age *(Plate 14)*. Behind this migration from the north were the Amorite kingdoms of northern Syria, while the major source of influence along the coast was Egypt. The political and economic influence of Egypt increased considerably during the 19th century, as is shown by the large number of Egyptian objects or imitations of Egyptian goods which have been recovered by archaeologists. Alabaster vessels and scarabs began to become common at this time. The Egyptian rulers and governors erected their statues in various temples throughout Syria and Palestine, and we have impressive pieces of sculpture from Ugarit, Qatna, Megiddo, Gezer, Tell el-Ajjul and other sites. One of the most interesting examples is the statue of Tehuti-hotep, governor of the Hare nome in Upper Egypt, who for a time was governor at Megiddo. It had been set up in the sacred area at Megiddo along with the statues of other rulers, and was found hidden in the *favissa* of a Late Bronze Age temple on the site *(Plate 9)*.

The period of Middle Kingdom rule in Palestine and along the Phoenician coast established a number of cultural patterns which continued until the end of the Late Bronze Age. Splendid temples and cult structures like those at Ugarit and Byblos were erected during this period and continued to be used, with minor modifications, to the end of the 2nd millennium. Particularly impressive is the Obelisk Temple at Byblos, on the site of an Early Bronze Age temple. This had a sacred area, with a cella in the middle of an open court and round this obelisks in Egyptian style bearing dedicatory inscriptions in hieroglyphic characters. These inscriptions, along with the royal scarabs of the rulers of Byblos, enable us to reconstruct the genealogy of the local dynasty. A number of the inscriptions name kings of Egypt, thus providing a means of synchronism between local chronology and that of Twelfth and Thirteenth Dynasty Egypt.

Cultic structures similar to those on the Syro-Phoenician coast are also found in Palestine during this period. At Nahariya in the northern coastal area, Megiddo in the Jezreel valley and Gezer in the Judaean foothills the same features appear, with stelae set round a central shrine. In the towns themselves there is evidence of urban planning : the town is surrounded by walls or ramparts and has a street grid, a sewage system, open squares, a royal precinct and residential areas for the ordinary people. The clearest examples are Megiddo and Tell Beit Mirsim.

New Political Conditions

Towards the end of the 19th and the beginning of the 18th century Egyptian control of Palestine and the Phoenician coast weakened. In northern and central Syria the mighty kingdom of Yamhad began to take shape at this time, with its capital at Aleppo. This kingdom was connected dynastically and through its Amorite population with the kingdoms of northern and central Mesopotamia (Assur, Mari and Babylon) ; and it also had commercial ties with Anatolia to the north, Mesopotamia to the east and northern Palestine to the south, which led to an interchange of cultural influences throughout this region. Along the Phoenician coast and in southern and central Palestine the later kings of the Twelfth Dynasty (to 1786 B.C.) and the earlier rulers of the Thirteenth Dynasty in Egypt (to 1720 B.C.) were still in control.

This period is known as the Mari period, after the Mesopotamian city of Mari, where large historical archives were found, including documents mentioning cities in Syria and Palestine like Aleppo, Qatna, Ugarit, Byblos, Hazor and Laish (the Biblical Dan). The region, which had previously fallen under the influence of the Orontes valley cultures, now came under the direct influence of the northern Amorite kingdoms. The excavations at Tel Dan and Hazor have revealed something of the culture of this period. The cities are surrounded by huge earthen ramparts, a form of fortification adopted from northern Syria, which in turn had borrowed it from Mesopotamia during the 20th century.

There is little doubt that Hazor was the most important city in Palestine at this time, with an area of some 800 dunams and a citadel on the south side towering over an extensive lower city to the north. On the east side a city gate built in Syrian style was brought to light. Within the upper city were the remains of a royal palace built during this period. This huge city, surrounded by its earthen ramparts, is very similar to Qatna and Qadesh, both in central Syria.

The Last Phase of Middle Bronze Age II

In the second half of the 18th century the last phase of the Middle Bronze Age (IIB) began to evolve. The transition was gradual, and most cultural features continued to develop. There were, however, a number of political changes which led eventually to a cultural break. The large and important cities which had been founded during the first phase of this period were abandoned. In Syria there are clear signs of decline and possibly even of a gap in occupation at Tell Mardikh (Ebla), Qatna and Byblos. In Palestine the large urban settlement at Tell Kabri, with an area of some 400 dunams, was almost entirely abandoned, and smaller towns like Tel Zeror and the Burga enclosure show signs of decline. Syrian pottery, which had come to this area in the way of trade, now disappears entirely and Tell el-Yahudiyah pottery types, rare in Middle Bronze Age IIA, become common. The destruction of Mari in 1759 B.C. and the death of Hammurabi in 1750 enabled the kingdom of Yamhad to gain control of much of northern Syria and south-eastern Anatolia, and possibly even parts of the upper Euphrates region. In the western province of this mighty kingdom Alalakh, a major city, has been excavated ; and stratum VII, which belongs to the period under discussion, has yielded the interesting plan of a North Syrian city of the end of the 18th century, surrounded by earthen ramparts and an outer glacis. Entrance to the city was through a monumental gateway flanked by three pairs of piers, with a dado of limestone orthostats. The gate gave access to an open space leading towards the royal precinct, a palace and its adjoining temple. Within the palace were two complexes — an official wing, decorated with frescoes, which included a reception room reached through a portico, with a staircase leading to an upper storey, and an administrative wing to the south with various service buildings. The temple, close to the west side of the palace, had massive walls up to 4 metres thick. It consisted of a porch and a principal chamber, and the objects found here included a number of statues reflecting the Syrian style of the Middle Bronze Age. This style, the beginnings of which can be seen in the statuary at Tell Mardikh (*Plate 6*), had a long course of development in northern and central Syria, continuing to the end of the Bronze Age. Along with the statuary were cylinder seals and other art objects of Syrian type, in a style which is a hybrid of local features, Mesopotamian influences and even Egyptian elements (*Plates 12, 13*) — for parts of Syria had been under Egyptian influence for some 200 years and had undoubtedly absorbed something of that culture.

Southern Palestine and the Hyksos

The traditional areas of Egyptian influence in the 20th-18th centuries B.C. — the Phoenician coast and most of Palestine — fell under Semitic rule during the 17th century. These Semitic rulers, who also occupied the Delta in Egypt proper, were known as Hyksos (Egyptian *hk3w h3swt*, "rulers of foreign lands"). To some extent they integrated the culture of the Delta region and southern Palestine, and so during the 17th century Palestine

46

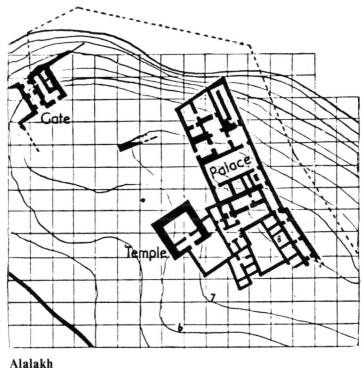

Alalakh
The Citadel of stratum VII

remained for the most part within the Egyptian cultural sphere. The farthest limit of this influence was in northern Palestine, in the Jezreel valley ; beyond this, at Hazor and Dan, the strong influence of North Syrian culture can be detected, apparently reflecting the limits of the political influence of the kingdom of Yamhad.

The finest Egyptian objects in Palestine are mostly luxury goods imported from Egypt or local imitations. There are four main groups of such objects : (a) scarabs, the personal property of persons of even moderate status, which

bore Egyptian and Canaanite motifs *(Plate 11)* ; (b) wooden boxes ornamented with bone inlays, mainly in Egyptian motifs *(Plate 12)* ; (c)
alabaster vessels, mostly of Egyptian manufacture ; and (d) faience juglets,
also mostly of Egyptian manufacture. Alongside these Egyptian elements
there are definite Canaanite and North Syrian elements in the architecture
and urban planning. Two examples of urban planning in this period may be
cited. One is the gate area and the complex of public buildings in Megiddo
stratum X — a gatehouse built in North Syrian style, like the gate in
Alalakh stratum VII, with an adjacent public building, from which an open
space led to the temple in the centre of the city. Next to the temple, as at
Alalakh, was a royal palace complex, and beyond this, to the south, were
private dwellings built on a uniform plan. This similarity between Alalakh
and Megiddo leads us to assume a uniformity of urban architecture in Syria
and Palestine at this time. The second example is the city of Tell el-Ajjul
stratum II, which, under very strong Egyptian influence, had residential
districts with a street grid, a drainage system and, in the centre of the town,
a palace or public building : a great labyrinth of courts surrounded by many
rooms. The considerable thickness of its walls indicates that this structure
was of several storeys. From the remains of this city great quantities of gold
objects *(Plates 16, 17)* were recovered, providing evidence of the wealth of
the period.

During the 18th and 17th centuries the inhabitants of Palestine and Syria
used two systems of writing, both of which were of foreign origin. In the
north, and later also in the south, we find the Mesopotamian cuneiform
script, with the Akkadian language as the literary vehicle ; in the south, in
Palestine and at Byblos on the Phoenician coast, the Egyptian hieroglyphic
script was in use. Initial attempts to simplify these complex scripts and
adapt them to suit the local dialects were already being made towards the
end of the Middle Bronze Age *(Plate 47)* ; the few " Proto-Canaanite "
inscriptions found in Palestine, like the inscribed sword blade from Lachish,
are clear evidence of this process.

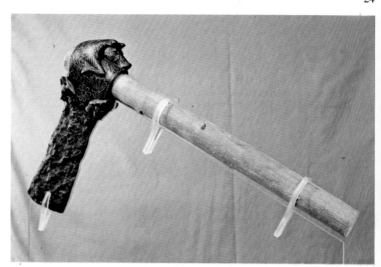

30

31

Near the end of Middle Bronze Age IIB, under the later Hyksos kings Khian and Apopi (end of 17th and early 16th century) a process of cultural transition set in, leading into Late Bronze Age I. Thus around the year 1600, still at the zenith of the Fifteenth (Hyksos) Dynasty, a number of new cultural elements appear in Syria and Palestine. In the central coastal region, between Ugarit in Syria and Tell el-Ajjul in southern Palestine, painted pottery of a new type, known as Bichrome Ware, began to be made. Certain of its basic forms are related to the pottery of the Middle Bronze Age, but the technique of ornamentation is entirely new. The surface of the vessel is covered with painted metopes on a buff ground, and within the metopes are geometric and animal patterns, including birds, fishes, stags and bulls *(Plate 18)*. Such pottery was to dominate Syrian and Palestinian production for some 150 years, and its appearance in the deposits at various sites offers a reliable chronological criterion for distinguishing between the end of the Middle Bronze Age and the beginning of Late Bronze Age I. Numbers of vessels of this type have been found in Egypt in contexts referable to the end of the Fifteenth Dynasty and the beginning of the Eighteenth (which succeeded the Fifteenth). With the Bichrome Ware there also began to appear large quantities of Cypriote pottery, some of the forms of which came to influence the Bichrome types. The abundance of imports from Cyprus at the end of the Middle Bronze Age and the beginning of the Late Bronze Age foreshadowed the inclusion of this island within the cultural and economic sphere of Syria, Palestine and Egypt.

THE LATE BRONZE AGE

1. LATE BRONZE AGE I

Historical Developments

In parallel with the cultural changes we have noted, but somewhat later, two historical events made a clear break between the Middle and Late Bronze Ages. In northern and central Syria the military campaigns of the Hittite kings Hattušili and Muršili I involved a series of destructions which can be dated to the end of the 17th and the beginning of the 16th century. In Palestine and along the Phoenician coast, and possibly also in southern Syria, a series of important cities were destroyed during the expulsion of the Hyksos dynasty from the Delta region in Egypt and the assertion of control over this region by the Eighteenth Dynasty (c. 1570 B.C.).

The first phase of the Late Bronze Age is well defined chronologically in both Syria and Palestine. In Syria it falls in the period between the destruction of Alalakh stratum VII and the building of Alalakh stratum IV (c. 1500 B.C.); and in Palestine it occupies the period between the conquest of Yahmes (1570 B.C.) and the campaigns of Tuthmosis III in Palestine and Syria (c. 1480). Culturally the first phase of the Late Bronze Age represents a continuation of the Middle Bronze Age; but there are a number of new pottery features, and some of the elements typical of the Middle Bronze Age now disappear. In the techniques of fortification the huge ramparts are no longer found, and stone- and brick-built town walls return to favour, though still based mainly on the defences of the Middle Bronze Age.

Art and Architecture

In the arts and crafts the objects made locally under Egyptian influence now tend to disappear, being replaced by objects actually made in Egypt or by local products with Canaanite motifs. In northern Syria a delicate painted pottery, known as Nuzi ware after its first find-spot, now came into use ; it stemmed from the Hurrian element in the population of Syria, and its first distribution was associated with the expansion of the Hurrian kingdom of Mitanni. In glyptic art, too, the Mitannian style replaced the Syrian style of the first half of the 2nd millennium. The phenomena noted here clearly reflect the rise to ruling status of the Hurrian element within the population and the end of the Amorite hegemony which characterised the Middle Bronze Age in Syria and Palestine.

In the realm of architecture the replanning of Alalakh by King Idrimi *(Plate 21)* in stratum IV is indicative of one of the most important elements of the early part of the Late Bronze Age. This planning was to continue on the same general lines in the Syro-Palestinian citadels throughout the Late Bronze Age and even into the Iron Age. An innovation can be seen at Alalakh in the separation of the palace from the temple and its transfer to the vicinity of the gate. The palace proper represents the first appearance of the type of building known to modern scholars as *bit-hilani* (though in ancient times this term was applied only to the portico of such buildings). This building, which undoubtedly was several storeys high, had a façade with a portico *(Plate 22)* and a staircase on one side leading to the upper floors ; beyond this were two spacious halls flanked by smaller rooms. During the Late Bronze Age and Iron Age this North Syrian building type became the regular plan for palaces in Anatolia, Syria and Palestine.

2. LATE BRONZE AGE II AND III

Historical Background

The second and third phases of the Late Bronze Age fall broadly within the 14th and 13th centuries. The second phase corresponds to the Amarna period in Egypt (c. 1400-1340) ; the third phase may well be connected with the end of that period, and should in part be considered a transition to the Early Iron Age (c. 1300-1200).

Imported pottery is an important aid to the establishment of an absolute chronology in this period, for from the early 14th century onwards Palestine and Syria were flooded with Cypriote and Mycenaean pottery. Of the two types the Mycenaean is especially important, for it can be related to absolute chronological data in Egypt, furnished in particular by the types found in the royal capital at Tell el-Amarna, which flourished only for a short period, and types found in precisely dated Egyptian tombs. This enables us to establish chronological and cultural synchronisms throughout the region — in Palestine, Egypt and the Aegean.

Politically the region was divided from the mid 14th century onwards between two major powers. In northern and central Syria the Hittite empire replaced the Mitannian kingdom, while on the Phoenician coast, in southern Syria and in Palestine Egypt still held sway.

The last two centuries of the Late Bronze Age were a crucible in which Canaanite culture crystallised out of the whole cultural pattern of the Syro-Palestinian region, including Egyptian elements borrowed during the Middle Kingdom, New Kingdom elements and features taken over from the Hurrian-Hittite art of northern Syria. In the pottery, too, we can observe the influence of foreign products on local wares, for Canaanite potters attempted to imitate the forms and ornamentation of imported Cypriote and Aegean vessels. The large scale on which pottery was imported, indeed, led to a decline in local production, and the quality of this is much lower than that of earlier local wares.

The Syrian Sites

In Syria two sites are particularly relevant to events within the Hittite empire — Alalakh and Ugarit. In Alalakh stratum III a Hittite fortress built in Anatolian style replaced the royal palace of the local dynasty. The sacred area continued in its traditional rôle, and in the series of Late Bronze Age temples there again appears, alongside the local type, the traditional Syro-Palestinian temple. This temple, built towards the end of the 13th century (stratum IB), shows close affinities with the Late Bronze Age temple at Hazor ; and the lions flanking the entrances to both temples gave them an even stronger resemblance. The existence of a temple of Syro-Palestinian type at Alalakh, in Hittite territory, towards the end of the 13th century, and of the North Syrian lions at Hazor, in territory under Egyptian control, at about the same time clearly shows just how far advanced was this process of cultural symbiosis in the Syro-Palestinian region, and reveals the uniformity of population which persisted in spite of its political division between the two empires. In addition to the series of structures described above Alalakh yielded an abundance of material bearing witness to the cultural wealth of the period : ivory vessels carved in Syro-Palestinian style, Egyptian faience vessels and, of course, Cypriote and Aegean wares.

The finds at Ugarit are also rich. In the sacred area the architectural traditions of the Middle Kingdom continue, while the royal palace, which had developed from a nucleus originally dating from the 15th century, was broadly similar to the stratum VIII palace at Megiddo. The Ugarit palace is built of dressed ashlar, a technique which became standard in public buildings of the Late Bronze Age. The significance of this palace lies in the discovery of the royal archives here, including literary works as well as political and administrative documents. Among other important finds were many vessels made of precious metals ; for the goldsmith's craft reached a peak at Ugarit, as is demonstrated by two bowls with Canaanite motifs *(Plates 25, 27)*. There was also a collection of ivories, one of the most important ever found on an ancient site in the Near East. Here for the first time appears a distinctively Canaanite style of ivory-working, which in spite of many Egyptian features already displays artistic independence and fine workmanship *(Plates 23, 26)*. This art, like the ashlar masonry of the public buildings, was to continue its development, reaching impressive heights during the Iron Age.

The Palestinian and Phoenician Sites

From the territory then under Egyptian control — that is, from Palestine and the Phoenician coast — an abundance of archaeological material has been recovered. Only a few outstanding examples can be mentioned here. At Hazor (Area H) a series of temples which yielded rich finds were brought to light, the earliest dating from the Middle Bronze Age; they present a parallel to the temples at Megiddo, even the plans of the structures being similar. In Area C a cult place was found with the *masevot* still in position *(Plate 29)*. At Megiddo, after its conquest by Tuthmosis III, the palace was transferred to its final location near the gate (stratum VIII); in form this structure is similar to the palace at Ugarit, the main halls of both having porticoes at their entrances. In the Megiddo palace there was a foundation offering of local and Egyptian objects in precious metals and ivory dating from the time of Tuthmosis III which have analogies in royal tombs in Egypt *(Plate 10)*. Above the stratum VIII palace were the later palaces of strata VIIB and VIIA, built on a similar plan. These were ornamented with frescoes, only meagre fragments of which have survived. In the stratum VIIA palace, dating from the end of the Late Bronze Age, was a large collection of ivories which had belonged to the ruler of the city; this collection is particularly important because of its variety — including local *(Plate 20)*, Syrian, Hittite and even Aegean pieces. Stratum VIIA still represents Canaanite Megiddo; it was destroyed by one of the Israelite tribes which penetrated into the region in the middle of the 12th century B.C.

At Beth-Shean, near Megiddo, there is an important series of temples beginning early in the Late Bronze Age (stratum IX) and ending at the beginning of the Iron Age (stratum V). The temple in stratum VII, built in the Egyptian style of the Amarna period, provided a significant historical and cultural synchronism, yielding a number of Egyptian architectural elements and various Syro-Palestinian objects *(Plate 19)*. Within the citadel at Beth-Shean were stelae erected by several Egyptian kings, clearly indicating that it was an important Egyptian fortress in northern Palestine.

At Lachish, in southern Palestine, there are a series of temples immediately outside the city, corresponding with the three phases of the Late Bronze Age. Here the abundance of Egyptian and local objects *(Plate 28)* reflects the close links between southern Palestine and Egypt, both culturally and also in population — for it must be remembered that in this period southern Palestine had been under direct Egyptian control for some hundreds of years, almost without a break since the Middle Kingdom.

Cultural Conditions at the End of the Bronze Age

In the final phase of the Late Bronze Age we find Syria and Palestine divided between two empires which at this time prospered in a state of peaceful coexistence and mutual assistance. This state of affairs, combined with the presence of an Amorite, Canaanite and Hurrian population throughout the Syro-Palestinian region, produced a broadly uniform culture.

This cultural uniformity was reflected in works of art in a distinctive local style, the clearest expression of which during this period was to be found in the art of ivory-carving. Most of the motifs and some of the techniques are derived from Egypt. Within the same cultural framework a uniform style of architecture came into being, mainly northern in origin. The plans of buildings are distinctively North Syrian : the ashlar technique, as used characteristically in the base of buildings, seems to have originated in this area.

In the Late Bronze Age urbanisation reached a very high level, and the towns excavated show evidence of planning, drainage systems and sewers, all indicative of considerable technical achievement.

Several different methods of writing were employed at this time. In the north, at Ugarit, the Amorites simplified the complicated cuneiform script and formed an alphabet of thirty characters, including some symbols for vowels. In the south, similarly, a Canaanite alphabet was evolved, using principles based in part on Egyptian hieroglyphs; this was at first pictographic, with twenty-five characters, and later, towards the end of the Late Bronze Age, developed into the archetype of the Iron Age alphabets used throughout the Mediterranean basin.

THE IRON AGE

III

1. IRON AGE I

The Coming of the Semi-Nomads

The 13th century was a kind of bridge between the Bronze Age and the Iron Age, and, as in earlier periods, the transition continued in Syria and Palestine over many decades. The process was not uniform throughout the region, generally beginning in the desert and the mountains and ending in the plains and valleys. The new period is known as the Iron Age, since it was at this time that iron came into use throughout the ancient Near East ; but in fact the widespread use of this metal does not go any farther back than the 11th century. The cultural changes which now took place were closely linked with movements of population — mainly from the fringes of the desert and the isolated regions of the central highlands. Nomadic and semi-nomadic elements fanned out, the Aramaeans in Syria, the Ammonites, Moabites, Edomites and the Israelite tribes east and west of the Jordan. The origins of these tribes are still obscure ; they seem to have been connected with the nomadic movements of the early 2nd millennium B.C., though they apparently did not take to sedentary life during the great wave of settlement which began in the 20th-19th centuries.

There is very little evidence from Syria, and until the beginning of the 12th century, when the large centres were destroyed, we have only occasional references in the documents to the *Ahlamu* (Aramaeans) in northern and central Syria. The picture is somewhat different in Palestine, for Israel seems to be mentioned for the first time as a tribal federation in an inscription of the Egyptian king Merneptah (c. 1220 B.C.), the *ante quem* date for the appearance of these tribes.

The evidence is more abundant in Palestine — in Galilee, the central and southern hill country and the Negeb. The archaeological material disagrees with the book of *Joshua*, the major literary source for events in Palestine during this period, in pointing not to a single conquest but rather to an extended period during which nomadic and semi-nomadic Israelite tribes settled on the fringes of the territories controlled by the Canaanite cities. Slowly, with the formation of larger and more numerous units, these new settlers came to control various parts of the country. The Israelite tribes, and apparently also the Aramaeans in Syria, first established themselves in unfortified settlements, bringing a type of pottery entirely different in form and technique from that of the Canaanites. Their houses, too, were of an entirely new character, representing the first appearance of the pillared house (known to modern scholars as the " four-room house ") which soon became the typical Palestinian dwelling. This type of house is found throughout the Iron Age, even in its latest phases *(Plate 31)*.

In upper Galilee many of the settlements of the first Israelite incomers have been surveyed, and one of them (Tell Harashim) has been excavated. In addition to the meagre architectural remains the excavations revealed a range of pottery very typical of the new inhabitants — jars with collared rims, crudely shaped kraters, jugs and juglets. There were also installations for casting copper, and the finds indicate that these settlers were adept in metal-working. In the Mount Ephraim area in central Palestine Israelite settlements have been brought to light at Shiloh and Bethel ; these were built over the ruins of Canaanite cities and contained pottery identical with that of the settlers in Galilee. Settlements were also established on new sites, like the two sites excavated in the southern Mount Ephraim area, at Ai and Khirbet Raddana, where the settlements dated from the initial stages of the Israelite penetration and had pillared houses of the three-room type. The pottery which dates these sites is identical to that found in the settlements in Galilee and the central Mount Ephraim area. In the southern Judaean hills and the northern Negeb we see an almost identical picture. Of particular interest are the initial Israelite settlements in the Beersheba region, which had not been occupied since Chalcolithic times. The Israelite settlement here is an indication of the density of immigration ; and the general uniformity in pottery and architecture points clearly to the unity of this wave of incomers.

The Sea Peoples

The first phase of Israelite settlement took place while Egypt was still in control of most of Palestine, and can be dated between 1250 and 1150 B.C. Towards the beginning of the 12th century a new phenomenon appeared which shook the very foundations of Hittite and Egyptian control in Syria and Palestine — a widespread invasion of peoples from the Aegean region, known as the " Sea Peoples ", who swept over the entire eastern seaboard of the Mediterranean around 1180 B.C. Within a relatively short time they had brought about the fall of the Hittite empire and the withdrawal of the Egyptians from most of Palestine. In northern Syria the invasion led to the destruction of many of the Bronze Age cities, some of which never recovered. Ugarit and Alalakh, the two most important centres, disappeared entirely from the scene, and many other cities were eclipsed for a time. In Palestine most of the coastal cities were sacked, especially those which lay on the invaders' route to the Delta in Egypt. In the Delta, however, the Sea Peoples were brought to a halt when they were decisively defeated by Ramesses II, and thereafter they were settled by the Egyptians in southern Palestine. The Bible and the Egyptian sources tell us that two groups of these Sea Peoples established themselves in this region — the Tjeker or Tjekel along the central coastal area and the Philistines in the south.

The influence of the Philistines in the cultural and political sphere extended far beyond the territories directly under their control, and the discovery of Philistine pottery in the early Israelite settlements in the central hill region should not be regarded as evidence of actual rule there. In the initial phases at least the pottery was imported from the coastal region. In the valleys, however, the Philistine material found in such cities as Megiddo and Beth-Shean certainly does reflect control by this people, even in the early phases. In contrast to the early Israelite pottery, which is rather monotonous and crude in form, the Philistine wares are in the Late Mycenaean tradition, and the forms are well developed, including kraters, rhytons and pyxides *(Plates 32, 33)*. The ornamentation consists of typical Aegean motifs, geometric and figurative, and is related to the Mycenaean IIIB and IIIC styles. The animals represented include the swan, which was popular among the vase-painters *(Plate 30)* ; generally depicted with outstretched wings, it appears on many types of vessel. Metal-work was another tradition brought by the Philistines from the Aegean world, and the development of iron-working in Palestine may well have been closely related to the activities of the Philistine smiths.

Of the central Philistine sites excavated we may note the important centre at Ashdod, where the initial settlement phase has been located above the remains of the Canaanite city. Farther north, at Tell Qasileh near the mouth of the river Yarkon, a settlement of Philistine foundation has been brought to light, with clear evidence of urban planning. In the district excavated it can be observed that in the second phase of settlement (11th century B.C.) the Philistine inhabitants adopted the three-room pillared house, evidently taken over from the Israelites. In recent work on the northern part of the site a Philistine temple has come to light, with an entrance chamber and a main hall, on the central axis of which were two pillars — a feature quite foreign to the temple architecture in Syria and Palestine ; it would seem that the origins of this plan are to be sought in the Aegean world. In the north of the country, at Megiddo, the Canaanite city of stratum VIIA was destroyed and replaced by an Israelite village with pillared houses (stratum VIB), which in turn was taken by the Philistines and replaced by a new adminis-trative centre (stratum VIA). This Philistine city was rebuilt on the general lines of the Canaanite town plan, the palace being again sited near the northern city gate. This is an unusual building with a large courtyard at one corner and a staircase on the west side. To the south of the courtyard were two parallel rows of rooms, with a corridor along the east side of each row. This structure is also without analogy in the architecture of Palestine, and its origins must lie outside the region.

An important find from this palace was the "Orpheus Jug", painted in traditional Aegean patterns and depicting Orpheus playing to wild animals.

The appearance of this motif in Philistine art is a further reminder of the links, both spiritual and cultural, between that people and the peoples of Iron Age Greece.

The Syro-Phoenician Area

The finds from Syria and Phoenicia which are ascribed to the period between 1200 and 1000 B.C. are very few indeed. In the northern coastal cities there are squatter settlements over the ruins of the splendid cities of earlier days, some of which died out altogether after a short time. The large Hittite centre at Carchemish on the Euphrates, on the eastern fringes of Syria, made a quick recovery, and a local dynasty arose to continue the Hittite-Luwian cultural tradition in northern Syria, developing the culture known as Neo-Hittite. Among the oldest monuments at Carchemish we may note those of King Asuhi — orthostats and statues, mostly pairs of lions flanking gateways and entrances — which are very similar in style to the Hittite art of Anatolia and northern Syria in the Late Bronze Age. This re-emergence of Hittite-Luwian elements is evident also on the northern borders of Syria, at Zincirli, where some of the early architectural finds belong to this period.

In the Amuq region, the territory of the earlier kingdom of Alalakh, we can clearly discern the difference between the Late Bronze Age and the Iron Age ; the earlier sites are abandoned, and new settlements spring up nearby. Thus a kilometre and a half from Alalakh there arose the capital of the Neo-Hittite kingdom ; at this Iron Age site, Tell Tayinat, rich archaeological levels containing important architectural remains were revealed. In the earliest stratum there was a large palace with complexes of courtyards and rooms, and adjoining this was a smaller palace built on the *bit-hilani* plan — the earliest example of this type in the Iron Age in northern Syria.

Farther south, at Byblos on the Phoenician coast, a royal tomb was found belonging to King Ahiram. Within the tomb was a sarcophagus, containing the king's body, with carved ornament and an inscription in a linear alphabetic script — the earliest found in Phoenicia — along one of its upper edges. The style of the ornamentation is a direct continuation of the ornamental art of the Late Bronze Age. The main motif is a representation of a king seated on a throne, with an offering table and women mourners in front of him *(Plate 34)* — apparently a depiction of an actual royal funeral. Certain elements of this representation appear in the Megiddo ivories, which date from the end of the 13th century *(Plate 20)*; we can thus trace a clear transition from the art of the Late Bronze Age to that of the Iron Age.

Towards the end of Iron Age I Syria and Palestine emerged from a period of transition and change, and kingdoms and political blocs began to crystallise. In material terms the earlier cultural centres, like the Hittite city of Carchemish and the Canaanite centre at Byblos, served as bases for the cultural development of the Aramaean and Israelite tribes in Iron Age II. The Philistine cities, whose inhabitants had brought with them evolved Aegean cultural traditions, also made a considerable contribution towards this development.

2. IRON AGE II

Chronological and Historical Considerations

Around the year 1000 B.C. Syria and Palestine entered a new cultural phase. At about this time the anarchy of the period of movement of peoples and destruction of cities came to an end and was succeeded by an era of political consolidation which had a profound influence on the events of the succeeding 450 years.

From now onwards the historical sources at our disposal become more numerous, providing us with reliable information, mainly on Syria. These sources are provided by Assyrian inscriptions, particularly the annals of the kings of Assyria, which make it possible to piece together much of the history of Syria during the first half of the 1st millennium. In addition we have the Neo-Hittite, Phoenician and Aramaean inscriptions. In Palestine the Bible still serves as the major source of information about events, but is supplemented by inscriptions, most of them discovered in recent years, in particular the ostraca found in excavations at Samaria, Lachish and Arad, which help us to reconstruct the historical processes in this region.

Iron Age II continued for some 450 years, and it is clear that this period should be further subdivided ; there are, however, several theories current on how this should be done, none of them free from problems. Most scholars now see a historical dividing line in the mid 9th century B.C., when Assyrian influence became the dominant political and cultural factor in Syria, while in Judaea and Israel there were dynastic changes, which in turn led to political and cultural developments. It is in fact quite difficult to see a clear-cut archaeological and cultural break in the middle of the 9th century, for earlier buildings and building styles continued in use with no essential modification throughout Iron Age II ; in the pottery and other small finds, too, there is nothing to indicate any significant change at this time — only the usual gradual development through the 9th century and the beginning of the 8th. Thus the most convenient method of subdividing Iron Age II for the purpose of dating and classifying the archaeological material is according to the century to which it is ascribed ; in case of uncertainty the designation " early " or " late " within Iron Age II is used.

The cultural uniformity within Iron Age II makes it possible to deal with the finds not only on the basis of their chronological ascription but also according to typological classification or site. In the typology of the pottery the situation is somewhat different, for the material can now be precisely dated to within fifty years. This method of dating is of course applied only when there are no better means of dating such as inscriptions, seals or other material of exact chronological significance.

Architecture and Urban Planning in Syria

In this period, as in the Bronze Age, the major influence on the architecture of Palestine stemmed from northern Syria. At the beginning of the period, indeed, the cultural influence of northern Syria gradually increased, and it would seem that certain general planning concepts were penetrating into Palestine at this time from this same source. In Iron Age II each local ruler established himself in his own citadel, which was generally patterned on the royal citadels in the larger centres ; indeed, there are numerous examples of this in the Syro-Palestinian region.

At Zincirli in northern Syria, capital of the Aramaean kingdom of Sam'al, the royal citadel of the 9th and 8th centuries B.C. has been excavated ; and here we find a number of principles of planning which had already emerged in the Late Bronze Age. The citadel was separated from the city proper and isolated from it by a wall ; the entrance to the royal residential area was through a series of gates designed to make access to the ruler difficult ; and the royal residence included a palace or palaces with adjacent service buildings. The royal citadel was situated in the centre of Zincirli and was reached by way of two gates, the lower walls of which were faced with ornamental orthostats. The upper part of the citadel contained the rulers' palaces — of which there were several, for each king added another palace to those of his predecessors and ornamented it with orthostats and inscriptions. Between the palaces, all in the classical *bit-hilani* style, were open spaces and courtyards. In the other parts of the citadel were store-rooms, stables, servants' quarters and barracks. The royal citadel of Zincirli did not change in plan from the mid 9th century to the end of the 7th century, when the Assyrian kings who had conquered the land of Sam'al added typically Assyrian structures, though without touching the main buildings of earlier periods.

80

46

47

48

49

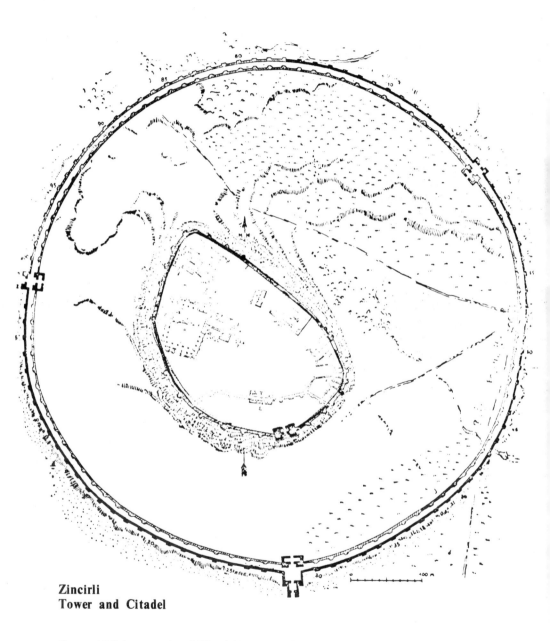

**Zincirli
Tower and Citadel**

Some 100 km south of Zincirli a very similar royal citadel was discovered at Tell Tayinat, apparently the site of Kinaluwa, capital of the land of Hattina.

The earliest stratum found here dated from the end of Iron Age I and was destroyed during the Assyrian campaigns of the mid 9th century. Over the ruins a new citadel was built, in which we can observe certain principles and details identical with those found at Zincirli. Here too the royal citadel was separate from the city proper, marked off by the entrance gateway and apparently also by a wall. In the royal complex three strata have been distinguished, associated with minor changes in the structures. On either side of a wide courtyard were two *hilani* palaces, with their splendid entrance porches situated opposite one another *(Plate 35)*. The larger of the two was undoubtedly the royal palace, and adjoining this to the south was a temple, both the palace and the temple being decorated with frescoes. The two structures are quite different in plan : while the palace had a broad-room entrance of *hilani* type, the temple had a long-room entrance with two pillars on lion bases *(Plate 36)*. This latter type of structure had a long architectural tradition behind it, stemming from Bronze Age Anatolia. The palace and temple have frequently been cited as analogies to the royal citadel built by Solomon in Jerusalem in the mid 10th century : a suggestion based on a comparison of literary sources on Jerusalem (the Bible) with the architectural finds at this site many hundreds of kilometres away. There is, indeed, weighty evidence for North Syrian and Neo-Hittite influence on architecture in the Israelite kingdom — not surprisingly, for during the 10th century two major powers came to the fore in the Syro-Palestinian region — the Neo-Hittite kingdoms in the north, with their long Hittite tradition, and the new Israelite kingdom in the south. The Phoenicians and Aramaeans, now caught between these two powers, were mere political dependencies, which served as agents of a process of cultural osmosis between the two powers, particularly from north to south.

At Tell Tayinat there are also indications that in the second half of the 8th century the palaces of *hilani* type were replaced by new structures in the Assyrian style. But here — very differently from Zincirli — the early citadel was destroyed and the palace of the Assyrian governor was built on a different part of the mound. The contemporary Neo-Hittite site at Hama (the Biblical Hamath), farther south, also contained a citadel, situated on the edge of the mound, but the architectural remains are insufficient to allow reconstruction of the plan. The central palace shows similarities with the large palace at Tell Tayinat, and adjacent to it is a gate, possibly a separate entrance from the city into the citadel.

The palaces, temples and other public buildings of the Neo-Hittites in northern Syria were ornamented with many reliefs carved on orthostats set along the lower walls. This art, largely a direct continuation of North Syrian and Anatolian art of the Late Bronze Age, disappeared in the 8th century and was replaced by official Assyrian art. Syria now became a province of the Assyrian empire, and local artistic and architectural creativity fell to a low ebb.

Architecture and Urban Planning in Palestine

A number of citadels similar to those noted in northern Syria were built in Palestine under the United Monarchy. In recent years parts of the citadel of Megiddo, built in the reign of Solomon (second half of 10th century B.C.) have been re-examined. Here two palaces in the North Syrian *hilani* style were built on opposite sides of the site. The entrance to the city was by means of a gate very similar in style to the gates of the Bronze Age but differing from them in detail (a direct entrance between three pairs of piers; two towers in front of the gate; ashlar foundations and base). This distinctive structure has made possible the identification in recent years of a number of other cities re-fortified by Solomon's engineers. Thus the citadel at Hazor, consisting mainly of the royal fort and auxiliary structures *(Plate 37)*, is also ascribed to this period; an identical gate has been identified at Gezer; and it has recently been established that the same type of gate was built at Ashdod in Philistia, slightly before the time of Solomon. This appears to indicate that these gates were not specific to the structures erected by Solomon, and that the plan and building technique were probably taken over from Israel's neighbours.

A new architectural element in the palaces built during this period in Palestine is the "Proto-Ionic" capital, in the form of a lotus blossom *(Plate 38)* — a type of capital which stems from Egyptian architecture of the Late Bronze Age, where it is found particularly on pilasters. In Palestine, and apparently also in Phoenicia, it appeared in the 10th century, and thereafter, until the end of the Iron Age, it was the typical capital in this region. From there it spread to Cyprus and Ionia, where it was to develop into the Ionic capital of classical architecture.

In the stratum above the imposing citadel built by Solomon at Megiddo a no less splendid administrative centre was built in the reign of Ahab (stratum IVA). Typical features of this were long pillared structures which were used as store-rooms and stables. In the last third of the 8th century, following the Assyrian conquest, the same changes took place at Megiddo as had occurred in the citadels of northern Syria, and Assyrian courtyard buildings, the seat of the Assyrian administration (stratum III), were built over the Israelite structures.

At Samaria, which was founded at the beginning of the 9th century, parts of the royal citadel have been brought to light. So far only remains which escaped the destruction wrought by the builders of later periods have been found, but it is possible to discern in the excavations a casemate wall of unique type, certainly belonging to the citadel. In the centre of this area stood the palace, apparently not of *hilani* type, and adjacent to it were various auxiliary structures. No gate leading from the city into the citadel has been found ; nor is it certain that all the buildings within the citadel have been located. The ashlar construction and the Proto-Ionic capitals which became prominent features in architecture from the time of Solomon onwards were standard in the buildings at Samaria.

In Judaea a number of important cities have been excavated. The first excavations in Jerusalem were carried out during the 19th century, and throughout the present century there has been much further work. The considerable destruction wrought by later periods, however, has almost entirely obliterated the Iron Age structures, and the architectural remains of this period are meagre. In recent years, however, the extent of the city on the west side has been clarified, and it is now evident that as early as the 7th century it had extended over most of the western hills. The necropolis of the local aristocracy of the Monarchy period, to the east of the city, was investigated in the early stages of modern archaeological research, and the tombs found here show clear evidence of Phoenician and Egyptian influence in architecture. At Ramat Rahel, near Jerusalem, a small royal palace-fortress was excavated ; it is dated to the 8th or 7th century and contains such impressive architectural elements as Proto-Ionic capitals and splendid ashlar construction. A unique find here was a window balustrade, built in the form of four small Proto-Ionic capitals ; such balustrades were known previously only from representations on Phoenician ivories from Samaria and Nimrud *(Plate 39)*. In southern Judaea a border fortress was excavated at Arad, revealing among other things a small temple, apparently for the use of the garrison *(Plate 40)*. This temple — still an isolated phenomenon in Iron Age II — includes elements borrowed from the temple architecture of the Late Bronze Age. The fortress of the district capital at Beersheba, near Arad, has also been excavated in recent years, and in this well planned 8th century city a gateway was discovered the upper part of which had been crenellated. Nearby was a store-room complex essentially similar to the one at Megiddo. Inside the gate, towards the centre of the fortress, was an open space, with the governor's palace beyond. The remainder of the fortress area served to accommodate the garrison and the ordinary citizens of the town *(Plate 41)*.

The dating of these various structures was made possible in most cases by the associated pottery and other small finds. At some sites (e.g. Arad and Lachish) the excavators were even more fortunate in discovering ostraca *in situ*, thus assisting them to establish precise dates for the structures.

Pottery and Art Objects

The pottery of the Iron Age is not rich and variegated like that of the Bronze Age. There is an impression of mass production throughout, and the forms are monotonous, with the minimum of ornamentation. Local variations between northern or "Israelite" types and southern or "Judaean" types can be distinguished. Some of the Cypriote and Phoenician pottery imported into the interior of Syria and the kingdoms of Israel and Judah stands out from the mass; it usually had geometric ornamentation and was undoubtedly related to the Proto-Geometric and Geometric styles in contemporary Greece *(Plate 42)*. Towards the end of Iron Age II, in the late 7th century, imported Aegean pottery again begins to appear along the Phoenician and Palestinian coasts — mostly Greek pottery in the "Wild Goat" style. Pottery of this kind has been found at Tell Sukas on the Phoenician coast, Mesad Hashavyahu on the southern Palestinian coast and even at Tell Malhata in the northern Negeb. Here we see the beginning of a flow of imports which was to increase steadily in the 6th and 5th centuries.

The ornamental art of the Iron Age found expression in the same fields as that of the Late Bronze Age. Ivory carving remained one of the principal creative arts, and many ivory objects were exported or taken as booty to the cities of the Assyrian empire. One of the largest assemblages of ivory objects of this period — part of the treasures contained in the palaces of the kings of Israel — was found at Samaria *(Plates 44, 45)*. In this collection, alongside ivories with traditional Egyptian motifs, carved in high relief, we find pieces which continue the traditions of Canaanite Bronze Age art *(Plate 45)*. This is particularly evident in a small group of ivories with animal motifs carved in the round *(Plate 44)*. In the engraving of seals a true Phoenician-Palestinian school developed, of whose work we have many hundreds of examples. Most of these seals are oval scaraboids bearing the name of the owner *(Plates 46, 48)*. Here we see the final adaptation of the Egyptian scarab as a stamp seal, and the almost complete abandonment of the Mesopotamian cylinder seal, which was still quite common in the Late Bronze Age. The motifs on the seals are also mostly of Egyptian inspiration ; but there are also representations of various animals, apparently totem-like symbols of the owner or his family. To judge by the names and titles inscribed on these seals, most of them seem to have belonged to royal officers or members of aristocratic families.

In the material remains of Iron Age II many elements from previous periods are interwoven. Trends which were strongly marked in the Bronze Age generally continued in the Iron Age. The Phoenician coastal belt, which in consequence of its busy trading activities was subject to Egyptian influences, in turn passed such influences on in the luxury goods and art objects which it exported to other countries — to central Syria, Israel and even Judaea.

THE PERSIAN PERIOD

IV

The conquest of Syria and Palestine by the armies of Persia in the mid 6th century B.C. brought these countries into a vast empire which ruled the greater part of the then known world. This region, which had hitherto been part of a more limited sphere, now became a land bridge between Egypt — one of the most important provinces of the empire — and Mesopotamia and Persia.

SYRIA AND PHOENICIA

In Syria the picture drawn from the archaeological evidence is a fairly vague one. There are considerable structures at various sites along the coast, and at Amrit, Tell Sukas and Byblos there are Phoenician temples which are ascribed to this period. The most important of these temples is the one at Byblos, on the traditional site dating back to the early days of the Bronze Age. The style of the temple is local, but we can already see Greek influences at work. At Sidon a number of walls and many architectural fragments from the palace of the local Persian governor have survived ; the fragments include capitals carved in the form of bulls' heads, as well as typical column bases, all of which clearly show that the source of inspiration for this structure was the royal palace at Persepolis.

A large number of anthropoid sarcophagi have been found throughout Phoenicia and on the Palestinian coast, reflecting the Egyptian influence on burial customs in this region. An outstanding example is the black granite coffin of King Eshmunazar of Sidon, with the lid carved in a likeness of the king in a distinctly Egyptian style. The coffin bears an inscription recounting the achievements of the dead ruler.

The ties between Phoenicia and her colonies in the Mediterranean are reflected in the abundance of Greek products found in the region. Attic pottery represents the largest percentage of the domestic pottery found in the Phoenician coastal cities, as well as at sites in the interior, in Galilee, Samaria and even Judaea.

The appearance of a new type of statue can also be attributed to influence from the Phoenician colonies. Limestone statues in archaic Cypriote style have been found in various parts of Phoenicia and Palestine ; they closely resemble contemporary archaic Greek statues. Alongside these splendid figures we find more popular types made in terracotta ; in style they can be divided into two groups, the one showing Western influence and affinities with the Cypriote statues, the other closer to the local style of the Iron Age *(Plate 49)*.

THE PALESTINIAN SITES

Excavations in Palestine are constantly supplementing our knowledge and throwing light on the culture and population of this region. The evidence points to a cultural polarisation during the Persian period : there seems to have been a striking difference between the culture of Judaea, Transjordan and the southern part of the Mount Ephraim area on the one hand, and that of the coastal plain and the northern part of the country on the other. These diversities are clearly seen in certain characteristics of the respective material cultures, no doubt reflecting differences in population. In the north and along the coast the population was Phoenician and Aramaean, while in the south and in Transjordan it was Judaean, consisting partly of people who had returned from exile in Mesopotamia and partly of those who had remained on the land.

Of the major sites of the Persian period we may note particularly Hazor, in the north, where there are remains of a fortress generally similar to the fortresses of the Assyrian period. In the centre of the structure was a spacious courtyard surrounded by large rooms, and to the south of the court were two additional rows of similar rooms. This plan is very close to that of the Persian palace at Lachish, one of the most interesting buildings found in

Palestine, which still included a central hall with a *hilani* portico. This is the last instance of such a building in the Syro-Palestinian region. It may be noted that the bases of the columns at the entrance are of a design which already shows Greek influence.

In the northern coastal area two cities were founded, apparently by Phoenician settlers — at Tell Abu Hawam, near the mouth of the river Kishon, and Shikmona, at the southern end of Haifa Bay. Excavations at these sites have revealed a planned urban layout and have yielded an abundance of finds indicative of their importance as ports. In Judaea the excavations of recent years have revealed a plethora of sites identified by the pottery and other finds as belonging to the Persian period. All of them are poor in architectural remains, except the site at En-Gedi, where substantial private dwellings of the 5th century B.C. have been brought to light. One of these houses, apparently belonging to a wealthy family, has a plan showing the influence of the traditional Mesopotamian courtyard house, and was at least two storeys high. This type of plan seems to have been brought in by the returning exiles.

In the Persian period more than at any other time we can see within the material culture of Syria and Palestine the influence of the surrounding world. We can detect in the metal-work strong influences from Egypt, Mesopotamia — brought mainly by the returning exiles — and Persia, the ruling power. We see very little Iranian influence, that little being mainly in metal-work, which came in as imports *(Plate 50)*. The most significant influence, however — and the most remarkable — was that of Greek culture. The coastal region of Syria and Palestine was now gradually becoming part of the Cypriote-Aegean sphere. This phenomenon, initially reflecting only economic power and cultural superiority, prepared the way for the inclusion of Syria and Palestine within the cultural framework of the classical world in later periods.

CONCLUSION

CULTURAL TRENDS

Looking back over the 1800 years of material culture in Syria and Palestine, we can trace a number of trends. In general there is a flow of influences from two directions. From northern Syria and Mesopotamia influences spread southward along the Orontes-Litani-Jordan river axis, and from the opposite direction they surged up from Egypt through southern Palestine and along the Phoenician coast. The Syro-Mesopotamian influence was mainly in the field of architecture, while Egyptian influence can be detected particularly in art objects and other small finds. Local cultural development also went on within the Syro-Palestinian region, but the powerful influence of the surrounding empires always left a profound imprint on local achievements.

Though this region tended, culturally speaking, to be provincial, a number of unexpected developments did take place here, perhaps as a result of the more unsophisticated approach of the provincial mind. An example is provided by the alphabet — a simplification of the fairly complex systems of writing used in the neighbouring cultures. This phenomenon can also be seen in the development of the minor arts. Local artists took over certain major concepts from the monumental art of their great neighbours, but also achieved independent styles which were quite remarkable in themselves. There were similar achievements in spiritual matters, but this is a large subject which is beyond the scope of the present study.

METHODS AND RESULTS

The results of the archaeological excavations which have provided the major basis for our survey have been accumulated by a century of fieldwork in Syria and Palestine. In spite of the great historical importance of northern and central Syria we have seen that archaeological investigations in these areas have been meagre, particularly in comparison with the intensive work done in Palestine. Along the Phoenician coast, too, many sites still await the archaeologist's spade ; indeed, the Phoenician culture of the Iron Age is largely known to us from goods exported to Palestine or Cyprus and subsequently brought to light there.

In Palestine itself modern archaeology is at a crossroads, and a lively scholarly controversy over the methods applied in the past and the appropriate methods for the future is still under way. The age of large-scale excavations in which large tracts of a site were exposed has come to an end, and a period of much more limited financial support has set in, compelling archaeologists to turn to more efficient means of interpreting the smaller quantity of data recovered. But even with the advance of archaeological methods it is still a basic precept that in order to discover and interpret the archaeological evidence it is necessary to expose large areas of a site ; for in small spot excavations scattered over a site only a local, fragmented picture can be obtained. We must hope, therefore, that substantial areas of many more of the mounds in Syria and Palestine will be opened up in future investigations.

Another form of research which has been somewhat neglected in recent years is the regional project, in which, instead of concentrating on a single site, an entire region containing many mounds and smaller sites is investigated. Thus instead of recovering the cultural history of a single locality the archaeologist can obtain an overall picture of an entire region and provide broader perspectives for interpreting its history and its culture.

CHRONOLOGICAL TABLE

Middle Bronze Age I (MB I)	2200/2100-2000/1950
Middle Bronze Age IIA (MB IIA)	2000/1950-1750
Middle Bronze Age IIB (MB IIB)	1750-1600
Late Bronze Age I (LB I)	1600-1450/1400
Late Bronze Age IIA (LB IIA)	1450/1400-1300
Late Bronze Age IIB (LB IIB)	1300-1250/1200
Iron Age I (Ir I)	1250/1200-1000
Iron Age IIA (Ir IIA)	1000-850
Iron Age IIB (Ir IIB)	850-550
Persian period (P)	550-332

All dates are B.C. and are approximate. The so-called " middle " chronology is adopted here and in the text.

Part II

From the Time of Alexander the Great
to the End of the Roman Period (332 B.C. - 324 A.D.)

Michael Avi-Yonah

INTRODUCTION

THE CONTRIBUTION OF GREECE AND ROME

In order to assess the impact of classical culture on Syria and Palestine it is necessary to take a few steps back in history. The first lasting contacts between Greece and the East were established in the second half of the 5th century B.C., after the Persian wars. Travellers (the most famous of whom was Herodotus), mercenaries and merchants traversed the East and sometimes settled there. They confronted an ancient and inert Oriental civilisation ; for the Assyrian and Babylonian conquests in the preceding centuries had effectively broken the political will of the Syrian and Palestinian cities, and this made the task of succeeding conquerors considerably easier. As long as the only vital force left to them — that of religion — was respected, the peoples of the East were ready to submit to any power. In conformity with their feudal and dualistic ideology, the Persians were not interested in propagating their culture and thus filling the Near Eastern vacuum. They left this task to the Hellenistic monarchies.

In 332 B.C. political power in the Near East passed from Persia to Alexander, and Hellenism began to penetrate the Orient both from below and from above. By the end of the 4th century conditions in Syria and Palestine had been stabilised. From 301 to 198 the Seleucids ruled the north (Syria) and the Ptolemies the south (Palestine), with Phoenicia divided between the two. At the beginning of the 2nd century the Seleucids succeeded, indeed, in uniting both areas ; but their power was by then already in decline, and the shadow of Rome was falling over the East. The gradual disintegration of the Seleucid empire led to a native Oriental reaction which almost extinguished Hellenism politically. The Hasmonaeans conquered most of Palestine, while the Nabataeans and Ituraeans contended for the rest of Syria. Hellenism was saved by Roman intervention, and the frontier between East and West stabilised on the Euphrates. It stayed there for the next six centuries.

58

59

60

71

72

73

74

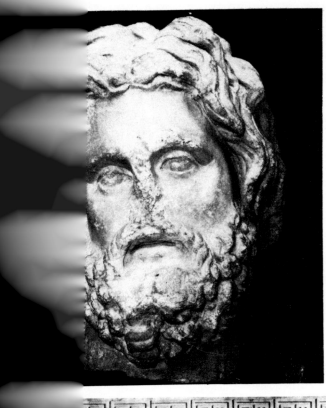

75

76

77

81
←

82
→

85 →

83
←

84
→

Classical civilisation in the Orient was mainly urban. Ancient cities were hellenised and new ones founded, with Macedonians and Greeks forming the basic stock of their population. Both types of city were focal points from which Greco-Roman culture radiated into the countryside, as is attested by the remains of temples, villas and civil engineering works. Archaeological evidence of this process is also to be found in the planning of the new towns or of new districts adjoining older foundations. The newly built temples were given the outward shape of Greek sanctuaries, but the interiors were still laid out in accordance with the requirements of Oriental theology and liturgy. There was less change in private houses, for the homes of the Greeks in their own country were not very different from those of the Orientals, both stemming from the common Mediterranean type built round an interior court. In some cases a Greek type *andreon* was combined with an Oriental *gynaeceum*. The Oriental gods adopted the outer aspect of their Greek counterparts, with whom they were syncretistically linked.

Greco-Roman culture in Syria and Palestine was marked by a steep rise in material standards of living. The release of the hoards of gold and silver which had been kept out of circulation by the Persian kings was one cause of this ; another was the large-scale application of the improvements in public administration and technology achieved by the Greeks under Aristotelian impetus ; a third was the stronger policing of the desert borders.

Rome added the one element lacking in the picture — the establishment of the *pax romana*. The result was a rapid expansion of the cultivated area into the steppe : the " sown " now gained on the " desert ". Political stability also made possible the extension of the profitable caravan trade across the desert.

One consequence of this increase of material prosperity in Syria was the possibility it offered of long-term planning and the erection of monumental buildings of gigantic proportions. The same process began in Palestine under the Herodians, but was cut short by the two Jewish revolts against

Rome. Only in the 3rd century and later is there evidence of a revival of prosperity in this area.

The transition from Roman to Byzantine culture was not marked by any drastic change. Some temples were turned into churches and a great many new churches were built. In Syria the great bulk of existing buildings continued in use, while Palestine benefited considerably from its elevation to the status of the Holy Land of the dominant Christian religion.

THE END OF THE ANCIENT WORLD

The decline which set in with the Persian and Arab conquests at first affected only the fringes of the desert. It accelerated as the Arab dynasties were superseded by the Seljuqs, Mamelukes and Ottomans; and the Crusades added their toll to the general ruin. In order to counteract possible sea raids the Mameluke sultans systematically destroyed all the coastal cities, with one exception. The towns and villages of the remote interior were abandoned to the bedouin, and the settled area shrank to parts of the coast and the adjacent hills. In the lowlands the breakdown of the elaborate Roman drainage system led to the formation of swamps. The harbours silted up. By the 17th century the material culture of Syria and Palestine had reached its nadir.

ARCHAEOLOGICAL RESEARCH IN SYRIA AND PALESTINE

I

1. THE REMAINS

From the Middle Ages to Modern Times

The revival of learning in Europe caused scholars to turn their attention to these ancient lands ; and in order to understand the form which their enquiries took we must try to visualise the state of the material remains of the past at that time. For this purpose we must imagine two areas of unequal width running from north to south. To the west were the regions which had remained inhabited throughout the centuries. Here the ancient structures had often been dismantled down to their foundations, which were subsequently covered over by accumulations of earth and sand ; other monuments were incorporated in later buildings. The tombs, unless of monumental proportions, had either been plundered or had been covered over and forgotten. The only visible ancient remains were structures of massive proportions like the temples at Baalbek or the Herodian walls of the Temple in Jerusalem.

The rest of the region — the southern and eastern parts of the Syrian steppe, the mountains in the Antioch area, the Hauran, the lands east of the Jordan, the Negeb — had been abandoned by their settled population and become the undisputed heritage of the bedouin. These tent-dwelling nomads did no deliberate damage to the ancient temples and houses, though they plundered the tombs. The only damage suffered by the remains in these areas was that caused by nature and by the failure to repair the ravages of sun and rain.

Throughout the Middle Ages Palestine, as the Holy Land, attracted much more interest than Syria. Pilgrims passing through the latter country were satisfied with noting down a few facts by the way, while reserving the full measure of their interest for the land of the Bible ; though even in Palestine they were usually only too ready to accept uncritically whatever stories they were told by ill-informed guides. It is characteristic of this state of affairs that the first reasonably factual report on Syria and Palestine came from a natural historian, Pierre Belon (1553). His successors Pietro della Valle (1616) and Richard Pococke (1735-42) covered larger areas but were much less scientific in their approach. Throughout the 16th and 17th centuries the interest of European classical scholars was concentrated on the ruins of Italy and Greece. The middle of the 18th century, however, saw a kind of breakthrough. Robert Wood visited Baalbek and Palmyra in 1753 on behalf of the Society of Dilettanti, and his volume of engravings gave European scholars for the first time some impression of the wealth of ancient remains on these sites. Although not always accurate, and somewhat given to romantic embellishments, Wood nevertheless recorded much that has since been lost.

19th Century Travellers and Scholars

During the 19th century the exploration of Syria and Palestine became both more intense and more scholarly. Two travellers, Ulrich Seetzen (1802) and J.L. Burckhardt (1810-12), penetrated deep into the Judaean and Transjordanian deserts. In 1824 and 1852 Edward Robinson travelled extensively in Palestine and Lebanon, and his critical intelligence swept away many cobwebs in the field of Biblical and later topography. He was followed by Titus Tobler (1835-65) and Victor Guérin (1865).

In Syria and Lebanon the next great wave of exploration was a consequence of the Druse massacres in 1860 and the French expedition which followed in their wake. Ernest Renan, the most famous of the new explorers, carried out researches in Phoenicia and Galilee ; and although his main interest was in Semitic and Biblical antiquities he also contributed to the interest in, and knowledge of, classical remains. W.H. Waddington, who travelled in Syria in 1861-62 after exploring Asia Minor, was mainly interested in epigraphy. M. de Vogüé (1864-77) disclosed an unsuspected wealth of architectural remains still standing in the Hauran and the hinterland of Antioch. The parallel explorations of Humann and Puchstein led to the excavation of Baalbek. In general the pioneers of the spade followed the early explorers almost too closely for the good of archaeology.

Organised Survey and Exploration

In the seventies of the 19th century the British Palestine Exploration Fund undertook a major survey of Palestine (1871-77), which was successfully carried out by Conder and Kitchener (the future Lord Kitchener). Although handicapped by insufficient knowledge of stratification and ceramic typology, the survey recorded a wealth of material, much of which has since disappeared. Supplementary surveys were undertaken east of the Jordan by Conder (1881) and Schumacher (1885-1902). The Negeb, with its six lost cities standing in the desert, was explored by Musil (1898-1902) and later by Woolley and Lawrence (1914). Southern Transjordan was thoroughly prospected for its Roman and Nabataean remains by Brünnow and Domaszewski (1905-07). In 1905 Kohl and Watzinger surveyed the Jewish synagogues in Galilee.

In the meantime the exploration of Syria did not stand still : indeed its greater wealth of visible surface remains made it a great attraction to explorers. At the turn of the century Butler surveyed the whole region east of Antioch from the Hauran to Philadelphia (1899-1900, 1904-09) ; and his competence as an architect preserved a thorough record of hundreds of dated buildings, thus making it possible to trace architectural development in Syria under Roman rule.

After the first world war the whole of Syria passed under French mandate, and the activities of the Direction des Antiquités during the period of mandatory rule included a systematic survey of the major ancient sites. Palmyra was surveyed and planned by Gabriel in 1925, Palmyrene by

Lassus. Tchalenko made a thorough survey of the villages in the Antiochene hinterland. The scattered antiquities of the Hauran were recorded and published by Dunand (*Musée de Soueida,* 1924). More recently (1958-59) Frézouls surveyed the theatres of Syria and Palestine.

From 1925 to 1931 Father Poidebard explored the Roman *limes* in Syria, developing the new method of aerial photography and following it up by confirmatory surveys on the ground. By this means large areas could be surveyed rapidly and remains invisible on the ground were revealed. This survey disclosed the existence of a complex network of roads (some passing through the uninhabitable Trachonitis), forts and fortified water points with which Rome had protected the province of Syria, and showed that the *limes* reached much farther into the desert than had previously been thought. Aerial exploration was also instrumental in revealing the *ager centuriatus* of Homs (1960), and was used in the investigation of the submerged remains of the ancient ports of Tyre and Sidon (1937-38).

In Palestine a survey of the whole of Transjordan was carried out single-handed by Nelson Glueck (1932-47), paying special attention to Nabataean sites. The state of Israel is now engaged in a complete archaeological survey of its territory, and parts of the Negeb and the coastal plain have already been investigated, using the latest archaeological methods.

2. ARCHAEOLOGICAL SITES AND EXCAVATIONS

The Primary Objectives

The conditions governing the preservation of ancient remains in Syria and Palestine are generally similar ; but the same cannot be said of the motivations of the archaeologists. In Syria the impetus was in the main antiquarian, and usually directed towards the most prominent periods at each site. In Palestine interest was from the outset directed towards Biblical antiquities ; the excavators were content to excavate the remains of later periods as an archaeological duty, performed with varying degrees of conscientiousness. One result of this attitude was that, on the whole, excavation began earlier in Palestine than in Syria. The first excavations were carried out in Jerusalem in 1864, when de Saulcy investigated the Tombs of the Kings (i.e. the Kings of Adiabene) under the mistaken impression that they were the tombs of the House of David. In 1867-70 Charles Warren carried out an excavation, under extremely difficult conditions, round the walls of the Herodian Temple. He believed, also mistakenly, that the masonry was of Solomonic date ; but his conscientious record of his findings preserved the results of his labours for posterity. The excavations in Jerusalem by F.J. Bliss (1894-97) were similarly marred by a mistaken chronology of masonry types. Bliss and Macalister's work on the tells of the Judaean Shephelah (1899-1900) brought to light among other things the Hellenistic stratum at Marissa and a late Hellenistic villa at Tell el-Judaidah, though the value of the results was diminished by haste in excavation and inadequate publication. In Macalister's excavations at Gezer (1902-09), however, every object found was recorded. Here too the remains of the classical period were only of incidental interest to the excavator.

In Syria the decision about where and what to excavate was governed by more objective considerations, the determining factor being the state of the remains themselves. The great cities on the Phoenician coast had been continuously inhabited down the ages, and were therefore regarded as archaeologically unprofitable. This did not, however, apply to their cemeteries ; and in fact the earliest excavation recorded in Phoenicia was of tombs near Sidon. In 1855 the cave of Magharat Ablun was investigated, and in 1887 Théodore Reinach and Hamdi Bey excavated the royal tombs of Sidon with their magnificent sarcophagi, including the Sarcophagus of the Mourners and the so-called " Alexander Sarcophagus ". On the whole, however, excavators working in the Syrian coastal area preferred to deal with the tells of pre-classical times. Byblos, where the Roman remains were exposed incidentally, was an exception.

The archaeological effort in Syria, then under Ottoman rule, was mainly in German hands. It was directed towards Baalbek, where the massiveness of the remains made them accessible even though they stood on the fringes of a modern township, and, farther afield, to Palmyra, where there had been practically no recent settlement. Baalbek was excavated in 1898-1905 (by O. Puchstein, B. Schulz and D. Krencker), Palmyra in 1902 and 1917. Archaeological activity on these two major sites was resumed during the French mandate and has continued ever since. At Palmyra the Service des Antiquités excavated the agora between 1924 and 1939, the triumphal arch was restored in 1932 and the cella and doorway of the Temple of Bel in 1933, while the excavation of the surrounding tombs led to an ever increasing number of discoveries. Particularly notable was the splendid tomb of Jarhai, discovered in 1936.

After the end of the French mandate work was resumed at Palmyra by the Syrian Antiquities Service, which directed its attention to the theatre, the colonnaded main street and the necropolis, where the discovery of 22 new hypogaea (including one dated to 88 B.C. and one of the 2nd century A.D.) was reported in 1960. A Swiss expedition led by P. Collart worked on the clearance of the second main temple at Palmyra, dedicated to Baalshamin (1954-56), and a Polish expedition directed by K. Michalowski (1959-63) excavated large sections of the so-called Camp of Diocletian, as well as several tombs with associated towers and hypogaea.

Restoration work was carried out at Baalbek between 1927 and 1935, and was resumed in 1941 with the clearance of the large many-tiered altar in the main court of the temple of Jupiter Heliopolitanus. In 1961 the two free-standing columns in this court were re-erected and their dates established.

Other Syrian Sites

The period of the French mandate also saw three major undertakings on new sites. One was the excavation of Antioch by Princeton University, which lasted from 1932 to 1939 ; but here the vastness of the site proved too much even for the best equipped expedition. The excavators did, however, clear a circus and a temple, four baths and a number of private houses. Their greatest triumph was the discovery of an unbroken series of mosaic pavements dating from the early Roman to the Byzantine period and including some of the finest mosaic work ever brought to light.

Another Syrian city, the ancient Apamaea, was excavated by a Belgian expedition between 1929 and 1940, revealing evidence of Roman urban planning of an advanced type.

The excavations at Dura Europos on the Euphrates arose out of one of the romances of archaeology. In 1921 a British officer noticed a frescoed wall in the ruins of a site then known as Es-Salihiye. He alerted Professor J.H. Breasted of Chicago ; but when Breasted arrived he was told that the military post established on the site was to be given up and that he had only 24 hours to complete the record. However, the hastily collected evidence, published as *Oriental Forerunners of Byzantine Painting,* ultimately led to a series of archaeological investigations of the site. The first expedition (1922-23) was directed by Franz Cumont, and his work was continued by Michael Rostovtzeff and F.E. Brown on behalf of Yale University and the French Académie des Inscriptions. In nine seasons of excavation (1928-36) almost half the city was exposed and fourteen temples were excavated, in addition to the famous synagogue and the earliest extant church. The remains included scores of private houses, shops and four baths, while among numerous public buildings were the praetorium, the palace of the *dux,* four barracks and the complete town wall with its gates. Dura, situated on the Euphrates and passing from Roman to Parthian hands and back, represents a mingling of Hellenistic and Oriental elements, although it was founded by Seleucus Nicator and its original population stock was Macedonian. Along with Palmyra, it enables us to study the gradual extinction of classicism in Syria.

The existence of a few very extensive sites should not lead us to overlook the numerous smaller excavations carried out from 1922 onwards, some of them producing material of prime importance. The search for, and discovery of, painted tombs continued almost without interruption in the coastal sector, from Tyre to Massyaf. A series of villas near Beirut and Baalbek yielded some fine Roman mosaics. In 1944-45 Lauffray took advantage of urban redevelopment in Beirut to study the forum of the Roman city and adjoining areas. Finally the excavation of a favissa at Amrit by Dunand (1945) and a deposit of terracotta figurines at El-Kharayib by Chéhab (1951) supplied most important evidence on the transition from the Persian to the Hellenistic period.

Excavations in Palestine

We now return to Palestine. Here the excavations at Samaria (Harvard University, 1908-11, directed by G.A. Reisner; resumed in 1931-37 by J.W. Crowfoot), although primarily directed towards the Israelite remains, nevertheless cleared Herodian and later levels with the painstaking methods developed in Egypt. After the first world war Palestine passed under British mandate, and the conditions for archaeological research improved considerably. As before, most of the effort was directed towards the Bronze and Iron Ages; but the excavators had by now a much clearer idea of the stratification of each site and were better prepared to deal with the remains of later periods.

The earliest major undertakings after the war were the excavations of the British School in Jerusalem, directed by John Garstang, at Ascalon (1920-22) and Dora (1923-24). On the former site a Roman *bouleuterion* was the main discovery, at Dora a Hellenistic harbour and temple. From 1921 to 1933 Pennsylvania University excavated at Beth-Shean (Scythopolis), finding among other things a Hellenistic temple. The work of the Görresgesellschaft, directed by Mader, at Mamre (Ramat el-Khalil, 1926-28) yielded a Herodian enclosure. An expedition from Yale University excavated Gerasa in Transjordan from 1928 to 1934 ; the result was a fairly complete picture of the layout, architecture and history of a caravan city of the Roman period. Excavations at Beth-Zur (1931-32) revealed the existence of a Hellenistic-Hasmonaean fortress. From 1936 onwards the Palestine Exploration Society (later the Israel Exploration Society) excavated an extensive Jewish cemetery at Beth-Shearim. In the course of the excavations, directed by B. Mazar and later by N. Avigad, nearly thirty catacombs of different sizes were found, in addition to a synagogue and a basilica. The burials dated from the 3rd-5th centuries and included the presumed tombs of the Jewish patriarchs. These Jewish remains represent only one facet of the country's sub-classical culture : the other aspect is represented by the Nabataeans, whose culture was gradually clarified by the excavations by G. and A. Horsfield at Petra (1936-37) and by the excavation of the Nabataean temple of Et-Tannur (N. Glueck, 1937) with its remarkable architectural sculpture.

Excavations in Palestine were interrupted by the second world war and the political crisis which followed it, but with the relative stabilisation of life from 1949 onwards archaeological activity was resumed in the two states which now shared Palestine, Israel and Jordan. One of the most urgent tasks for archaeologists in Jordan was the following up of the sensational find of the Dead Sea scrolls in a cave near Khirbet Qumran ; and this site was excavated by R. de Vaux and L. Harding in 1949-53, revealing an Essene "monastery" of a unique kind. On the Israeli side these discoveries led to the Judaean Desert Expedition of 1960-61. A mass of objects and documents dating from the end of the Bar-Kokhba revolt (135 A.D.) was found by Yigael Yadin. Hellenistic (Hasmonaean) and Roman remains, including a bath, were excavated at the nearby site of En-Gedi (B. Mazar and others, 1960-65). Other work in the southern wilderness of Israel included the excavation of the Nabataean and Roman cities of Eboda and Mampsis (Kurnub), carried out by Avraham Negev from 1956 onwards. In 1963-65 Yadin completed the clearance of the desert rock fortress of

Masada, with its wealth of Herodian and Zealot material. In Transjordan the excavations of P.W. Lapp at Iraq el-Amir (the ancient Ammonite city of Birtha), the stronghold of the Tobiad rulers of Peraea (1961-62), revealed the principal building, the Qasr el-Abd, to be a Hellenistic temple in mixed classical and Oriental style. At Petra G.R.H. Wright and P. Parr have been working on the clearance and architectural definition of the monuments. Finally the work done at the two rival capitals of the country, Jerusalem and Caesarea, deserves mention. In Jerusalem Kathleen Kenyon conducted a series of excavations from 1960 onwards, finding Herodian and Roman remains as well as earlier levels. At Caesarea an Italian expedition (A. Frova, 1959-64) cleared the Herodian theatre and established the line of part of the Herodian city wall. Another expedition (S. Yeivin, 1951) excavated a late Roman town square decorated by statues of an earlier period. Michael Avi-Yonah and Avraham Negev cleared the area of the synagogue and found adjoining it the remains of the Hellenistic tower of Straton, the precursor of Herodian Caesarea.

3. METHODS AND AIMS

The early beginning of excavations in Palestine was inevitably reflected in a lower standard of scientific precision. It would be unreasonable to expect from these early archaeologists the refined methods of a later period ; and allowance must also be made for the very great difficulties with which these pioneers sometimes had to contend. We may think, for example, of the heroic efforts of Captain Charles Warren, who was compelled to explore the walls of Herod's Temple in underground tunnels, since the fanaticism of the Moslem authorities prevented him from carrying out any work on the surface.

Alternative Approaches

In general we can distinguish two schools among the early archaeologists. One was derived from German and Italian experience, gained from work at

Pompeii and later excavations, and was developed by Wilhelm Dörpfeld at Troy, Olympia, Pergamon and other sites. This school, whose protagonists were mostly trained as architects, can be called the architectural school. Excavators working with this method concentrate on the remains of buildings, first exposing walls by trenching and then tracing floors, wall openings, etc., on the alert for any signs of rebuilding or other changes and for fragments of architectural ornament (capitals, column bases, friezes, cornices, etc.). This method, which was used in the excavation of Baalbek and Palmyra, enables the excavator to deal fairly rapidly with large building complexes. Its advantages are most evident in dealing with buildings whose date is known from literature or from inscriptions ; but it must be admitted that such apparently certain information is sometimes misleading. The dating of Baalbek to the Antonine period on the basis of a passage in Malalas, for example, has now been generally abandoned. Nor are inscriptions always conclusive. And in cases where the development of a series of buildings has to be established by excavation, this method rarely produces the desired result, unless combined with a careful tracing of sections.

The other school, which can be called the Anglo-American school, was based on the discovery by Flinders Petrie in the nineties of last century of the evidential value of pottery. Sherds of different periods differ so significantly that they can be used as dating indicators once a proper sequence of styles has been established ; and accordingly pottery artifacts, with their ubiquity and indestructibility, have become the mainstay of archaeological stratigraphy. This is particularly true on mounds where the strata are numerous and the remains of superimposed levels of masonry few and indistinct.

Theory and Practice

In dealing with the massive remains of classical antiquity the excavator is confronted with problems fundamentally different from those faced by archaeologists concerned with earlier periods. One such problem is the conservation of the remains brought to light. This is hardly a problem in the case of the architecturally insignificant structures of the Chalcolithic, Bronze and Iron Ages. The remains of the classical period do, however, warrant careful restoration ; and the systematic excavation of ever deeper levels until virgin soil was reached would destroy their educational and aesthetic value. Moreover the application of the stratigraphic method in its full rigour is ideally possible only in prehistoric caves, where a year's work is measured in square metres : it has to be considerably modified in the excavation of structures extending over many thousands of square metres.

As we have seen, large-scale stratigraphic excavations were almost entirely lacking in Syria until the twenties of this century, and the new methods of work were thus mainly developed in Palestine. At Gezer Macalister used a sequence of parallel trenches and excavated the mound in slices, the spoil from each slice being used to fill the immediately preceding trench. This is a rapid and thorough method, but it is entirely dependent on the exact recording of the various levels and their equation between one trench and another : otherwise the excavated area is left in complete chaos. At Samaria Reisner combined for the first time the trenching method with the use of sections, and his methods were later generally adopted.

The modern stratigraphic method has been applied in all subsequent excavations in Palestine and Syria. At Dura Europos the necessity of clearing entire blocks of buildings militated to some extent against the exact recording of details ; and at Antioch and recently at Palmyra, where modern methods were applied, progress has been tantalisingly slow. In general the excavator of a classical site must in some degree combine the two methods if he wishes to obtain satisfactory results.

A separate methodological chapter could well be devoted to the problems of excavating tombs. Here slow and painstaking work is often rewarded by a wealth of everyday objects such as are lacking in the remains of large public buildings. Although usually found robbed, the tombs of the classical period may contain paintings and sculpture which escaped the attentions of the plunderers: the wealth of the Palmyrene cemeteries, for example, is proverbial. One difficult problem is the ever-present menace of the illicit excavation of tombs — though the curators of most museums would sadly admit that most of their finest exhibits are the product of this reprehensible practice.

Results and Problems

Since archaeology is basically the handmaiden of history, we must ask ourselves what contribution the excavation of classical sites in Syria and Palestine has made towards solving the historical problems of the Hellenistic and Roman periods in the Orient. As we are now dealing with periods in which the art of historical writing was fully developed we need not depend on archaeology to supply us with a historical framework, as in earlier periods : at most we can look for some confirmation of a historical development, some modification of the accepted *res gestae* or a more detailed insight into matters — in the field of economic or religious history, for example — which are usually contemptuously dismissed or taken for granted by the ancient historians. We need think only of the profound implications of the finding of the Dead Sea scrolls on the religious history of the crisis which accompanied the rise of Christianity. In the main, however, the " voice of the monuments " is of greatest value in providing evidence on developments in the fields of art history and cultural life in general. Here the various trends can be analysed and traced to their sources ; we can observe the modifications they underwent in a foreign medium ; and we can elucidate the process which led to their final extinction.

The particular problem which confronts us in Syria and Palestine is the impact of Greek art and architecture. Although neither of them produced an original art which can be measured by the standards of Egypt or Mesopotamia, the influence of these two great centres of Oriental art, together with a third centre of lesser importance in Asia Minor, dominated their cultural life. The art of Syria and Phoenicia, and to a lesser extent that of Palestine, is a reflection of Egyptian, Mesopotamian, Hittite and Neo-Hittite, Assyrian and Persian trends. Conforming to the tenets of all Oriental art in its traditionalism, its linear character, its expressionism, its verism, its hierarchical arrangement, its stylisation and its *horror vacui*, it was now confronted with an art based on entirely different conventions — on the conservation of organic form and a concentration on the essential in composition. Greek architecture was based on a series of set rules in the development of the trabeate style, which it had brought to as high a degree of perfection as Greek sculpture had brought the anatomical exactitude of representations of the human form and Greek painting the creation of an optical illusion conforming to visual perceptions.

The history of Hellenism in the Orient is the story of the gradual imposition of these artistic concepts on the peoples of the East, and of the modifications and amalgamations which the pure vision of Greek art underwent in the process. In Syria and Palestine we have in particular to consider the counter-trends of Parthian art and the attempts of the peoples living on the border between the two worlds to create an individual compromise, and the difficulties of adapting Greek art to the deeply rooted aniconism of the Jews. In the following chapters we shall attempt to trace these developments, beginning with architecture and then proceeding to discuss in turn sculpture, painting, mosaic-working and the minor arts.

ARCHITECTURE

II

1. URBAN PLANNING

Hellenistic Town Plans

The Hellenistic and Roman periods saw an uninterrupted succession of building activities in which later constructions were continually being superimposed on earlier ones. There are, therefore, few remains of structures which we can confidently assign to the Hellenistic period. There is one element, however, which no later building could entirely conceal, though it might occasionally distort it — the town plan. Towns founded in the Hellenistic period were laid out on a planned grid, commonly called Hippodamian. The grid was always adapted to local conditions, but in itself it is unmistakable. Moreover it differs sufficiently from later Roman town planning to enable us to identify it.

The essential elements of the Hellenistic town plan are two longitudinal streets, one of which serves the agora or main market place. These two streets are intersected at right angles by numerous cross streets, of a width which varies according to their importance, and there are also a number of streets running parallel to the two main longitudinal streets. This network divides the whole area of the town into blocks of equal size.

An example of this Hellenistic town plan is to be seen at Dura Europos. Although the Hellenistic buildings of this city were rebuilt in Parthian and Roman times the essential street network was preserved. The agora in the centre is situated between the two longitudinal streets, one of which could be carried along for its full length, while the other had to take account of the two deep valleys which project inland from the river front. Two similar valleys defended the northern and southern sides of the city wall, while one of the inner ravines served to protect its acropolis. The main cross street ran from the Palmyra gate in the centre of the western city wall, which protected the most vulnerable part of the town, past the agora to the second

145

longitudinal street and then changed its direction to reach the river gate on the east side by way of one of the ravines. The residence of the chief magistrate of the city, the *strategos,* was on a spur overlooking the ravine, with the temple of Zeus Megistos behind it. Another important temple, that of Artemis, faced on to the agora.

Another Hellenistic town plan has been recovered by a study of the layout of present-day Damascus. Here too, as also at Antioch, it was found that the modern network of streets still in the main followed the ancient pattern. In Damascus the rectangular town area, situated between the two rivers Abana and Pharpar, was laid out round two long streets, one of them the " street which is called Straight " of *Acts* 9, 11, which ran past the theatre and the royal palace. The parallel street had to take account of the position of the city's principal temple, that of Jupiter Damascenus — probably an old sanctuary of Hadad — which could not be moved. This second street ran straight to the agora, which it intersected.

A minor example of a Hellenistic town plan was brought to light in the uppermost stratum of Tell Sandahanna, the ancient Marissa, in south-western Palestine. Here too we find the two principal streets, with the agora between them, intersected by a number of parallel cross streets. The agora is surrounded by civic buildings, and a whole block nearby is occupied by a double caravanserai. Marissa was a Hellenistic administrative centre, inhabited by hellenised Sidonians and Idumaeans, which later fell into the hands of the Hasmonaeans, when the population adopted Judaism. It was destroyed by the Parthians in 40 B.C. and never rebuilt — a fact which accounts for the preservation of its Hellenistic remains. This history explains the disintegration of the Hellenistic layout which can be observed in the plan.

Other Hellenistic foundations in the East have not been sufficiently explored to establish their plan. We can only presume that both Antioch, capital of the Seleucid empire, and the new Antioch which the hellenising Jews planned on the western hill of Jerusalem were laid out on the same lines. In the great city of Antioch the royal palace — like the acropolis at Dura — was built on a separate geographical feature, in this case an island in the river ; and the elongated shape of Seleucus I's city readily lent itself to double axial planning. In Hellenistic Jerusalem the Acra or acropolis was separated from the rest of the city by a small valley — another parallel with Dura. We may note in passing that Hellenistic town plans outside Syria, as for example at Alexandria and Ptolemais in Cyrenaica, followed the same general principle of double axiality.

Apart from the town plans there are hardly any remains of Hellenistic architecture traceable in Syria or Palestine. The foundations of peripteral temples have been found at Seleucia, Beth-Shean and Dora ; but since only the foundations have been preserved little is known of their structure — though at Seleucia there is evidence of the use of the Doric order.

Roman Town Plans

The political and economic effects of Roman rule in Syria and Palestine are generally regarded as having been beneficial, apart from the destruction wrought in Palestine by the two Jewish Wars (66-70 and 132-135) and the effects of the great Imperial crisis of the 3rd century. Many factors created a favourable soil for architectural progress : the general pacification of the East, the expansion of trade with the eastern countries (in which Syria's neighbours to the east, the Palmyrenes and Nabataeans, had a profitable share) and the development of an extensive network of roads. Particularly important in this respect was the construction of the Via Nova by Trajan between Damascus and the Red Sea, which was a major factor in the prosperity of Gerasa and other Transjordanian cities.

As soon as we begin to analyse the architecture of the Roman period, however, we are confronted with a considerable semantic difficulty: how much of Syrian architecture can properly be called Roman ? The whole of the eastern part of the Roman Empire was Greek-speaking, apart from the native languages which still lingered on, and derived its artistic inspiration from Hellenistic models. There are indeed indications that some of the architectural features of the period were influenced by Roman art as it had developed in its homeland of Italy. The question remains, however : to what extent were these Roman elements in their turn derived from Hellenistic prototypes ?

In the field of urban planning we can point with certainty to one type of plan which is purely Roman — the layout of some of the cities planned as Roman colonies. This plan, based on the pattern of a Roman camp, took the form of a square intersected by two main streets, the cardo and the decumanus, which cut across the town at right angles to one another between gates set in the middle of opposing sides. This basic plan is found at Beirut (Colonia Julia Augusta Berytus from about 15 B.C.), where the cardo, flanked by fora, temples, a basilica and the famous Law School, inter-sected with the decumanus and a theatre adjoining the northern forum completed the civic centre. A similar arrangement can be seen in Jerusalem (Colonia Aelia Capitolina from 135), where the layout of the Roman colony still determines the street plan of the Old City. The architects of Hadrian's reign who planned the new colony had, however, to allow for some deviation from the standard plan, since the ruined Herodian Temple and the valley on its west side necessitated the doubling of the cardo and a discontinuity in the line of the decumanus. The plans of Baalbek (Colonia Julia Augusta), Bostra (Colonia Nova Traiana Bostra, 106) and Philip-popolis (232-237) conformed to the standard scheme.

The Colonnaded Street

Contemporary with this somewhat rigid and military style of planning is another type of urban plan, much more subtle and sophisticated than either

the Hippodamian or the colonial type. Probably originating in the Hellenistic East, it first appears in the time of Augustus and Tiberius, and was
followed at Petra and Gerasa in the 1st century, at Palmyra about 110 A.D.
and at Apamaea in the late 2nd century. Its latest descendant was the plan
of Constantinople in the 4th century. This type of plan was based on a
colonnaded main street running lengthwise along the city. It was not usually
laid out in a straight line, but consisted of a number of sections meeting at
varying angles, according to the lie of the land and the positioning of the
main public buildings. At the junction of two sections there was a circular
open space, also surrounded by columns, with a tetrapylon or other suitable
monument in the centre. Triumphal arches were set at the beginning of the
colonnaded street and sometimes along its length, and the colonnades which
ran along the whole length of the street were interrupted by arches at the
points of intersection with the cross streets. There was usually a secondary
street parallel to the main one, and whenever necessary colonnaded streets
branched off in the direction of some monument or feature of the landscape.
The advantages of this type of plan were its flexibility, the multitude of
interesting and varied vistas it afforded, the commercial advantage of lining
the main street with shops under the colonnades, and not least the
opportunity it offered for adorning the numerous columns with statues of
the city's benefactors.

It is probable that the earliest city to be planned on these lines was Antioch,
even though the archaeological evidence for the dating of its main street is
not clear. It may even owe its origin to Antiochus IV, who built a new
district, Epiphaneia, on the slopes of Mount Silpius and may well have laid
out the new main street to link his foundation with the older city of
Seleucus I. At any rate we know that Herod of Judaea paved the street and
provided it with colonnades (Josephus, *Antiquities,* XVI, 148).

When Herod proceeded to lay out his two new cities in honour of Augustus,
Caesarea and Sebaste, he adopted the same plan. Caesarea was semi-oblong
in shape, with the main street running parallel to the coast from the north

gate to the theatre. Between this street and the harbour was a raised terrace for the Temple of Augustus, and the forum was presumably sited opposite it on the other side of the main street. At Sebaste the colonnaded street was planned with still greater skill, following the contours of the hillside and skirting the forum and the acropolis. It is likely that a second street followed the same pattern on the north side of the hill, but of this there is no archaeological evidence.

At Gerasa *(Plate 51)* the new town plan was evolved in the second half of the 1st century. It was based on a colonnaded main street running parallel to the river Chrysorrhoas, which bisected the city. The main street was twice intersected by streets leading to bridges over the river, the inter-sections being marked by tetrapyla. One of the city's temples stood at the south end of the street. Half way along its length the street ran past the great temenos of the principal temple, dedicated to Artemis, with massive propylaea *(Plate 52)* giving access to the temple on one side and to a wide street running down to the bridge on the other.

At Palmyra the line of the main street was determined by the great temple of Bel to the east, the theatre and agora in the centre and what may have been the civic centre (the palace of Odenath ?, later the so-called Camp of Diocletian) on the other side. The road was 1100 metres long from the temple of Bel to a tetrapylon, and 20 metres wide, and consisted of three sections set at an angle to one another. It had two branches, one leading from the theatre to the agora, the other running past the " Camp of Diocletian " in a southerly direction.

At Apamaea the cardo, dated to the time of Marcus Aurelius, was inter-rupted at regular intervals of 105 metres by arches leading into side streets.

2. RELIGIOUS ARCHITECTURE

Greco-Roman and Oriental Features

The spectacular group of temples at Baalbek (Heliopolis) *(Plates 53, 54)* reflect the influence of Rome in two different ways. It was the stability and prosperity brought about by Roman rule that enabled those responsible for building the temple — which was not merely a local but a provincial enterprise — to plan on such a grandiose scale. It now seems likely that the planning of the temple began in the time of Augustus and that the actual building continued into the reign of Caracalla, a period of two full centuries ; indeed it was never actually completed. We are reminded of the slow growth of the Gothic cathedrals. Rome's other contribution to the Heliopolitan sanctuary was the axial and symmetrical plan, which reflected ideas quite foreign to classical Greece but was certainly inspired by the Imperial fora. The architects may have been Greeks, but the spirit was that of Rome, with its striving after order, symmetry and grandeur.

If we consider the Syrian temples as a whole, we note a dichotomy not so much between what is Greek and what is Roman as between the classical and the Oriental ; or rather we have to draw a finer distinction between temples which conform in their external aspect to the Greco-Roman type, while accommodating their interior to the requirements of hellenised Oriental cults, and those which are purely Oriental in conception and planning but conform in the details of their external adornment with the prevailing fashions of classical architecture. The temples of Baalbek, most of those in Lebanon, the Gerasa temples and — so far as we can judge — the temples built by Herod at Sebaste and Caesarea belong to the former category ; the second group comprises the three great sanctuaries at Palmyra, Damascus and Jerusalem, the Nabataean temples at Seeia, Ramm and Tannur, and most of the surviving temples at Dura.

Classical-Type Temples and Synagogues

There is one feature of the first group of temples which may be due either to Roman or to late Hellenistic influence : we cannot be sure which. All these temples belong to the common Roman type of podium temple : even if peripteral in type, they stand on an elevation and are approached by a staircase in front. The second group shows much variety in this respect. The temple at Palmyra was a peripteral structure, but its entrance was marked by a wide flight of steps extending well outside the peripteros. In Jerusalem, on the other hand, Herod's Temple stood on a podium with a staircase in front.

In their external aspect the temples of the first group conformed to the canons of classical temple architecture. They were prostyle or *in antis,* with a triangular pediment and columns fashioned according to the accepted standards. But once we pass the threshold of the temple we notice a considerable difference between the interior of a classical Greek cella and that of a Syrian temple. In the former the divine presence was only hinted at, and the cult statue stood almost on the same level as the worshippers. In the East the divine immanence was felt much more strongly, and in order to emphasise this the part of the temple consecrated by the Presence was raised to a higher level and became an *adyton.* This elevated chamber is found in the earliest of the temples in Lebanon, at Deir el Qala and Qalat Fakhra (1st century). The concept achieves its full expression in the interior of the two great temples at Baalbek, where we find a reproduction of a small temple inside the large one, surmounted by a " Syrian " archivolt (an arch combined with a triangular pediment) and approached by a separate staircase.

This enhanced importance of the interior of the temple is marked by a series of columns engaged in the inside wall, one of the characteristic features of the Syrian temple from the 1st century onwards. The wall spaces between the columns are divided into superimposed rows of niches, each surmounted by a gable (arched or pedimental) in which statues could be set. In the largest temple of this type, at Baalbek, the arrangement of the interior of the cella is projected outwards into the great court *(Plate 56)*, along the sides of which, between its two flanking porticos, are rectangular or semicircular exedrae with engaged columns in their walls.

The architects of the Baalbek temples also deviated from the accepted standards of classical, and more particularly Roman, composition in another respect, interrupting the view of the façade of the great Temple of Jupiter by setting two altars on the axis of the court. The larger of these, built with Hellenistic stereotomy but in an Asiatic tradition, was 18 metres high, and must have completely blocked the frontal view of the temple façade.

Of the other two temples at Baalbek, the Temple of Bacchus, as it is commonly called *(Plate 56)*, is remarkable for its carved coffered ceiling, with representations of gods and the *tychai* of the various Syrian cities which contributed to the building of the temple.

While the architectural elements of both of these temples are more or less in conformity with classical standards, Oriental influences are clearly visible in the decoration, for example in the capitals and the carving round the doors, the friezes and entablatures of the adyton, etc. The gently moulded relief of classical Greece, which achieves its effects by the transitions between sculptured planes, is replaced by sharply differentiated areas of light and shade, an effect achieved by a lavish use of the drill. The result is a kind of openwork relief which is intricate and exuberant but pays less attention to beauty of line. There is also a noticeable tendency to stylise the floral exuberance by sharpening the angles of the trellises which weave all over the surface.

The use of light and shade effects is also apparent in the planning of the adyton. While the interior of the cella is kept in the dark, a blinding shaft of light strikes the sacred image.

The third temple at Baalbek, usually attributed to Venus, is an ornate circular structure with external niches, the curves of which are repeated in the podium. The preference for architectural curves became prevalent in Syria from the 2nd century onwards. It can be explained on the aesthetic level by the Oriental liking for the rich and sumptuous. Another possible explanation, based on religious symbolism, is the importance accorded to the arch and the rounded niche in emphasising the eminence of the deity enshrined within the curves.

Whatever the explanation, an increased use of the apsidal niche can be observed in Syria from the middle of the 2nd century onwards. In some cases, as in the Ed-Der temple at Hosn Suleiman in Lebanon, the whole temple becomes an apse. In others, as at Rahle, the adyton is built in the form of a horseshoe-shaped recess. At Slem the pattern of a Christian basilica is anticipated by an apsidal niche in the centre of the rear wall, with two lateral rooms flanking it. The apsidal niche reappears in 191 A.D. at Es-Sanamein and, in a slightly modified form (with diagonally sloping side walls), at Shuhba (Philippopolis). Another temple, at Atîl, contemporary with this last example shows the type of ceiling borne on a vaulted transverse arch peculiar to regions in which wood is scarce.

Another typical feature of the classical-style temples of Syria is the so-called " Syrian gable ". This appears in two forms : as an arch in the centre of a horizontal entablature, and as an arch in the base of the pedimental triangle. The former type can be seen at Seeia in the Hauran, where it dates from about 31 B.C. The other, more usual, form is found in Hellenistic buildings in Cyrenaica and at Pompeii ; and it was this form that became so common in Syrian architecture as to earn the specific name of Syrian gable. It occurs at Baalbek in the adyton within the temple, but in external use is found only on the propylaea, which date from the beginning of the 3rd century. It is a regular feature of temples in Lebanon and Syria from the 2nd century onwards.

We conclude our survey of sacred buildings influenced by classical architecture with a type of building — the synagogue — which we should not normally expect to find within this group. In doing so we anticipate the discussion of Herodian buildings in a later section. From the typological point of view, however, the synagogues of the earlier type (2nd to 4th century) in Galilee are strongly influenced by the temples of the Hauran : we have, indeed, epigraphical evidence that the architects who worked in the Hauran also worked in Galilee. The Galilean synagogues *(Plate 57)* are set on terraces, with a portico crowned by a Syrian gable and another gable of the same type over the façade of the whole building. They have three entrances in front, with an arch over the main entrance *(Plate 55)*. Windows and wall niches are surmounted by gables or conches. The main architectural decoration consists of ornate friezes *(Plate 58)*, probably from the interior of the building, executed in the style we have noticed at Baalbek, with much use of the drill, sharply accentuated contrasts of light and shade, stylisation of plant forms, etc. The use of images of animals and even of human beings, carved in relief, shows the liberal interpretation of the second Commandment current at that time among the Jews.

Oriental-Style and Nabataean Temples

We have seen that in many cases the Syrian temples were adapted to the rules of Hellenistic architecture, at least as regards the interior. There is, however, a class of temple, including some of the largest, most ancient and most venerated, in which the traditional Oriental arrangements had apparently to be preserved at all costs. The utmost concession that could be allowed to the prevailing fashion in architecture was the adoption of a Greek order of columns or Greek ornamental details.

One example of this type is the great Temple of Bel at Palmyra, planned in the reign of Tiberius but not completed until the Antonine period. The temple stood within a spacious enclosure which was surrounded by walls, pierced by windows, with a portico on the inner side. The sanctuary proper was elevated on a platform approached by steps and had a peripteros in the manner of a Greek temple ; but there the similarity with Greek architecture ended. The very long cella (127 metres) had a monumental portal on one of the long sides, following the plan of a Babylonian temple, and not one but two adyta, one at each end. There were windows in the long sides and staircases at the corners leading up to four turrets at the corners of the roof. The fashion for turreted temples is also attested by a series of smaller sanctuaries in the Hauran.

The second temple built in this style was the temple of Jupiter Hadad at Damascus. Here too the sanctuary was in the centre of a large temenos surrounded by porticoes, and inside this was a smaller court containing the temple proper and an altar in front of it. The Damascus temple, however, underwent so many changes (from temple to church and from church to mosque) that only its general outline can be established.

An even worse fate befell the third of the Oriental-style temples, the Herodian Temple in Jerusalem. In this case the literary evidence enables us to supplement to some extent the scanty material remains. Here too the basic dimensions were prescribed by tradition, though the architects were able to diverge from the rules about the height of the building, at any rate to a limited degree, by adding an extra storey, with no real function, to an otherwise low structure. Owing to the need to segregate the various classes of people who were allowed into the Temple a series of courts was built for the accommodation of Gentiles, women, Israelites and priests. The general plan of the Herodian Temple resembles that of the Palmyra and Damascus temples. Here too there was a shrine within an inner court, with an altar in front of it. The inner court and an adjoining secondary inner court were enclosed within a large outer court surrounded by colonnades, and the whole precinct was set within a massive outer wall. The situation of the Temple made it in any event a natural fortress, in which respect it differed from both Palmyra and Damascus.

The representations of Herod's Temple on the coins of Bar-Kokhba and in the synagogue at Dura Europos suggest a tetrastyle façade. The Biblical prescriptions obliged the builders to set the sanctuary on an east-west axis, with the main doorway in the end wall. The use of Corinthian capitals and the straight crenellated roof are reminiscent of Palmyra.

The Qasr el-Abd at Iraq el-Amir, the Tyrus of the Tobiad family of Transjordan, probably represents another type of Oriental temple superficially adapted to the exigencies of Hellenistic style. Its interior seems to have been divided into the traditional three parts of a Jewish temple (porch, sanctuary and holy of holies), with the addition of an opisthodomus at the rear. As in the Palmyra temple, there are staircases at the corners. The Doric epistylion is interrupted by the doorway and continued at a higher level, above an Orientalising frieze representing a procession of lions. Other Orientalising elements are the capitals in the interior, formed of two horses' heads with an eagle between them — reminiscences of Persian art combined with a Ptolemaic heraldic device.

The Nabataean temples are another type of sanctuary which combines an Oriental core with a Hellenistic exterior — a not inapt symbol of the whole religious situation in the Hellenistic East. Temples of this kind have been found at Seeia in the Hauran, Hosn Sfiri (Temple C) in Lebanon, and Tannur and Ramm in Transjordan. In each of these there is a square masonry core framed in walls with engaged pilasters, to which later additions gave the external aspect of a Hellenistic temple. At Ramm the temple was preceded by a portico and surrounded by a court with engaged columns round its inside walls, as in the interior of the Baalbek temples. At Tannur the inner shrine (dating from the 2nd century B.C.) was surrounded in about 8-7 B.C. by an enclosure wall with engaged pilasters surmounted by "Nabataean" capitals and a straight epistylion. The shrine itself was encased in masonry with an arch in front, flanked by engaged pillars decorated with carving. At the beginning of the 2nd century A.D. the whole temple was again remodelled. The shrine was given a new cornice and a new high altar, which was reached by a staircase to the rear. The façade of the inner court was embellished with higher pillars topped by Corinthian capitals, a pediment was set over the gate and the straight cornice was surmounted by an arched superstructure. Here again we note the gradual penetration of classical-style ornament, while the essentially Oriental character of the temple is unaffected.

3. PUBLIC AND PRIVATE BUILDINGS

It remains to discuss two further groups of structures, one of a public and the other of a private character, which, considered from another point of view, can be seen as presenting Hellenistico-Roman characteristics on the one hand and Hellenistico-Oriental characteristics on the other.

Civil Engineering Works

The first group comprises those major works of civil engineering which have always been the pride of Roman architecture and reflect Roman daring, lucidity and love of symmetry and order. In this category are included the Roman roads and the bridges, many of which are still in use. Allied to these are the city gates and triumphal arches, numerous examples of which have been found in Syria and Palestine, mainly dating from the Antonine period. Here we have Roman architecture at its purest, with the triple opening, the columns supporting the cornice, the niches between the columns above the side gates, and so on. There are examples of this kind at Gerasa, Palmyra and Bostra, and the so-called Ecce Homo Arch in Jerusalem also belongs to this type. The Roman architects often used such features skilfully to conceal changes in the line of the streets.

Along with the Roman roads we find Roman aqueducts and other types of hydraulic works. No city of any size in Syria and Palestine was left without an assured water supply, which might be conveyed over a distance of many kilometres *(Plate 62)*. The aqueducts sometimes supplied water to pools which could be used for the naumachies and other aquatic performances beloved of the Syrians. The conduits usually ended at public fountains (nymphaea).

Among major works of hydraulic engineering the tunnel cut by Vespasian and Titus to divert the waters of the river of Seleucia is one of the most remarkable. It consisted of several sections, one of which was 130 metres long and 7 metres high, with another section 80 metres long. The Roman engineers in charge of the work had two groups of labourers (among whom must have been many Jewish prisoners of war) cutting the tunnel from both ends, with a third group tunnelling down from above.

One of the purposes of the aqueducts was to supply the enormous quantities of water required by the public baths, another hallmark of the Imperial period. The baths which have been found throughout the territory of Syria and Palestine, from the capital city of Antioch to such modest little townships as Beth-Yerah on the Jordan, all conform to the standard type : an undressing room (apodyterium) is followed by the frigidarium with a pool of cold water, a tepidarium and finally a caldarium or hot room built over a hypocaust which was heated from outside.

As if to show that these amenities were not the exclusive prerogative of the Romans, Herod the Great provided for his desert fortress of Masada a series of aqueducts and baths unequalled throughout the area for engineering skill — and for the paradox inherent in the construction of six baths *(Plate 59)*, together with cisterns with a capacity of some 40,000 cubic metres, in an area with an annual rainfall of no more than 80 millimetres. To achieve this end twelve cisterns were cut, in two rows, and two aqueducts were constructed to supply them, one crossing a valley on a bridge and the other damming another valley. The number of baths at Masada seems to show an almost obsessive concern with bodily cleanliness.

159

Theatres

The third class of buildings which were clearly Greco-Roman in origin were the theatres and other buildings designed to house public performances. These show the same ubiquity as the provisions for water supply : no city, so far as we know, lacked a theatre, which could of course be used for other purposes such as public meetings. The performances given in these buildings no doubt ranged from classical drama to pantomime and aquatic displays. The structure may vary in detail or in size, but the basic features are the same. All the theatres in Syria and Palestine are of the Roman type, with a semicircular cavea, an orchestra and a raised podium. Often the stage is flanked by two towers, which served for the purposes of operating stage machinery. The theatres vary mainly in the use made of natural slopes wherever possible, in contrast with those built in their entirety.

The theatres were in constant use, as can be seen, for example, from the history of the one at Caesarea *(Plate 65)*, which was originally built by Herod and subsequently rebuilt at least twice. One unusual feature of this theatre in its earlier stages was the painted floor of the orchestra, which was apparently renewed annually. Many cities were not satisfied with a single theatre : Gerasa, for instance, had three, two inside the city and the third outside, adjoining a pool which could be used for aquatic performances. Theatres are known to have existed in Herodian Jerusalem, and they have also been found in such centres of Oriental culture as Palmyra and Petra.

The rear wall of the theatres, the *scaenae frons,* always had the elaborate baroque façade which we associate with the Hellenistic theatre. It had the conventional three doorways enclosed in a framework of columns, tier upon tier, with niches between them, the gables of the niches being alternately flat and curved. Higher up, the entablatures were given the full baroque treatment, with broken pediments intersected by curved lines or pavilions projecting from the wall. This fanciful arrangement was only possible where there were no considerations of statics to limit the free flight of the architect's fancy. The Syrian architects' delight in endless variety of architectural ornament found full vent in such structures, and the planning and ornament of the Syrian theatre façades are among the richest and most elaborate in the Roman world. The influence of this type of architecture was not, however, restricted to theatres. It appears whenever a high wall has to be decorated regardless of statics, as in the rear walls of the various nymphaea at Byblos, Philadelphia and Gerasa, and even in the tombs and temples at Petra, where the native tradition of rock-cut façades, as evidenced in its purity at Medain Salih, has been adapted to the decoration of façades incorporating features of the Hellenistic *scaenae frons*.

Houses and Palaces

If we now turn to the palaces and private houses of the classical period in Syria and Palestine, we encounter a fundamental difficulty in distinguishing between the Greek and the Oriental style of house. Both belong to the common type of Mediterranean dwelling, with the rooms ranged round an interior court. In this respect there is no difference between the houses of Delos and those of Palmyra or Dura. In both cases we find a concern to maintain the privacy of the interior : the entrance doorway hardly ever leads directly into the central court, but usually opens into a corridor adjoining it or into a series of rooms from which there is access to the court. The degree of elaboration of the entrance varies from west to east : the Palmyrene houses have a higher degree of privacy than those of Antioch or Samaria. In one case, at Tell el-Judaidah, we can clearly distinguish between two parts of the same house : one is built in the Greek fashion with a court surrounded by a colonnade, while adjoining it is another structure with a narrow entrance and its own court, perhaps a gynaeceum of Oriental type. One feature which distinguished the Greek from the Oriental style of house was the use of columns in the former, in contrast to the Oriental preference for a wide open *liwan* on one side of the court.

Two palaces of the Herodian dynasty demonstrate different approaches to the construction of the ruler's residence. One type, exemplified in the palace at Jericho, represents the ceremonial approach. The palace is situated in a park, surrounded by terraces round which flow canals. The building itself is laid out symmetrically round a large court, with a pillared hall on one side. The other type, more private in nature, is found at Masada. Here one palace, at the northern end of the rock *(Plate 60)*, is built on three terraces, one above the other, with a court surrounded by porticoes on the lowest terrace, a kind of circular belvedere on the middle one and a small four-roomed house, open to the north, on the uppermost terrace. The larger (western) palace has a large number of rooms, workshops, store-rooms, etc. *(Plate 61)*, but the main part, with two throne-rooms each approached through a *prostas* with two columns, is reached by way of a gate, a corridor and a large court, arranged asymmetrically, with no concern for the regularity and hierarchical architectural composition which we find in Roman or even in Parthian palaces, like the one at Dura.

4. FUNERARY ARCHITECTURE

Local Traditions and Hellenistic Influences

In this final section of our survey of Syro-Palestinian architecture we take leave of man's temporary dwellings and consider his permanent home, the tomb. The native tradition of burial in the Orient was the rock-cut funerary cave, which in the case of great families might consist of several adjoining chambers. In Phoenicia and northern Israel the tomb chamber was entered by way of a deep shaft. The graves of great men were marked by tall structures, often in the shape of towers or pyramids. In the Hellenistic period another type of tomb, possibly originating in Alexandria, became commoner — the loculus tomb, in which burial recesses were cut in the walls of the various chambers. This type of tomb is found at Marissa in the

2nd century B.C., and appears at Jerusalem in the second half of that century in the so-called " Tomb of St James ", which in fact belonged to the priestly family of the Bene Hezir. The importance of this tomb lies in the fact that in addition to its rock-cut Doric façade it shows traces of an obelisk-shaped *nefesh*.

In Syria a different tradition prevailed. Here we find a tomb at Suweda belonging to a man named Hamrath and dated to 95 B.C. — one of a long line of descendants of the Mausoleum at Halicarnassus. It has engaged Doric columns along the sides, a Doric frieze and a stepped roof (which may have culminated in a pyramid), and on the side walls are carvings of armour and shields. There are several other monuments of similar type in Syria and Lebanon : one at Qalat Fakhra, for example, has a high base surmounted by columns, two free-standing in the centre and two engaged in a wall, the whole structure being topped by a steep-sided pyramid. The same general shape is found in the monuments at Hermel, where the walls of the structure bear flat stylised hunting scenes. The influence of the most famous of Greek tombs (and its derivatives like the tomb at Cnidus) also made itself felt farther south. The " Tomb of Zechariah " in Jerusalem *(Plate 64)* is a plain cube with rock-cut engaged columns and pilasters along the sides and an Egyptian cavetto cornice, all surmounted by a rock-cut pyramid ; it is dated to the second half of the 1st century B.C. The so-called " Tomb of Absalom " *(Plate 63)*, with a circular tholos and a concave pyramid culminating in a flower, is dated to the beginning of the Christian era.

Tombs of the Roman Period

The other tombs round Jerusalem, dating from the early Roman period, are not marked by any prominent monuments but have rock-cut façades, usually with two free-standing columns between engaged pilasters. The frieze is sometimes in classical Doric style, but it is frequently interrupted by floral or representational symbols or combined with garlands. The pediment is decorated with a flat acanthus, flower and fruit ornament covering the whole surface. An exception to this type is provided by the " Tombs of the Kings ", the burial place of the kings of Adiabene in Mesopotamia, who adopted Judaism and settled in Jerusalem. Here there were several pyramids over the tomb, which was protected by a rolling stone and contained sarcophagi with stylised floral ornament in the Palmyrene manner. It should be noted that the very strict interpretation of the second Commandment in the time of the Second Temple forced the Jewish artist to avoid any representational elements except floral motifs ; he was of course free to use geometric patterns. While the sarcophagi of the well-to-do showed a preference for floral decoration, the plainer ossuaries of ordinary people were mostly decorated with geometric motifs (particularly six-petalled rosettes) which were drawn with compasses and cut with the sculptor's knife. The light and shade effects thus produced recall the drill-work of Palmyra and Baalbek.

The rock-cut tombs at Petra were subject to no similar restrictions on figurative representation. Here, however, the architects subordinated motifs of this kind to the overall designs of rock-cut façades of a strongly theatrical character (Plate 67). They could indulge themselves in designing fantastic pavilions set between light colonnades and broken cornices, concave roofs, etc., since they were free from considerations of statics.

Later Jewish tombs, like those in the necropolis of Beth-Shearim (3rd to 4th century), include a few constructed mausolea but are mostly rock-cut catacombs, each with a series of halls and burial chambers containing arcosolia. The most honoured burials were provided with a masonry façade containing three doorways built on to the rock face (Plate 68) and above this an open-air praying place. The coffins found in these tombs reflect a radical change of view in rabbinical circles on the use of figurative images. If no direct act of pagan worship is involved almost any representation of human figures, animals or birds is permitted (Plates 69, 70), including frankly mythological scenes (Plate 71). A similar change of attitude is observable in synagogues of the same period.

The tombs in the vicinity of Palmyra and Dura are again of a different type. The original form seems to have been a burial tower of several storeys, with the representation of a funeral banquet on the outside and stelae with busts of the deceased marking their burial places inside the tower. The earliest such towers date from the late 1st century B.C., the most sumptuous from 50-150 A.D. The best known is the Tower of Elahbel (113 A.D.), with an interior chamber surrounded by pilasters with Corinthian capitals; the ceiling of the chamber is decorated with carving on which traces of paint are still visible. Another famous tower-tomb is that of Yamliku (Iamblichus), built in 83 A.D., which had five storeys.

Recent excavations have led to the discovery of underground funerary caves associated with towers — a transitional type which was ultimately supplanted at Palmyra by the hypogaeum. Several of these underground tombs have yielded carved reliefs and busts, the value of which as archaeological evidence is greatly enhanced by the fact that they are well dated by inscriptions. The best preserved of these tombs is that of Jarhai, begun in 108 A.D. It consists of a main burial chamber ending in a double exedra, with steps leading down to it. The walls of this chamber are pitted with loculi, which were closed by stone slabs. At a later date two lateral exedrae were added, though only the one on the west side was completed. The rear wall of this is occupied by a representation of a funeral banquet; the lower part of the wall under this carving is taken up by burials, as are the side walls, each burial being closed by a slab with the bust of the dead man. It is clear that these tombs served whole tribes rather than families.

Another example of a large burial complex which illustrates the commercialisation of the funeral arrangements in Palmyra is the " Tomb of the Three Brothers " — Namain, Maale and Saadi, who had this hypogaeum cut in 160 A.D. They and their heirs (in 241 A.D.) sold part of the funerary cave to others, who in turn re-sold it. It seems that the tomb with its 390 burial places was constructed for sale, in the same way as a block of flats is built for letting at the present day, and that parts of it were acquired by funeral undertakers who dealt in single burials or groups of burials. The painted decoration of this tomb is of great interest to art historians : it includes mythological scenes (e.g. Achilles at Scyros), hunting scenes and images of Victory holding circular medallions with the portraits of the dead.

Before concluding this chapter a word must be said about the technical skill which is evident throughout the building activities of the classical period in Syria and Palestine. The builders of the period were especially expert in quarrying and transporting stones of a massiveness which still evokes our respect, particularly when it is remembered that they lacked modern sources of power. The trilithon at Baalbek — the three large stones in the foundations of the temple podium, measuring almost 20 metres in length and 4.16 metres in height — provides striking evidence of this ability. The same sense of massive effort is evident in the outer wall of Herod's Temple, with stones of up to 12 metres long *(Plate 66)*. This solidity of construction, found in most buildings whatever their scale, goes far to explain the preservation of the architectural remains of the period.

1. SCULPTURE

Sculpture, both in relief and in the round, but especially the latter, was an art in which the Greeks excelled to a degree never equalled before or since. It is not surprising, therefore, that the impact of classical sculpture was felt in the East even before the Hellenistic conquest, that it remained strong throughout the Roman period, and that classical sculpture lost its appeal only with the general change in the artistic climate in the 3rd century. Nevertheless there were always areas where the old Oriental traditions managed to retain a foothold. This is primarily true of the Jews, whose aniconic tradition precluded the representation of what was finest in Greek art, the human anatomy. But even nations free from the restrictions of the Jewish Law, like the Nabataeans and Palmyrenes, were — mainly, it seems, for reasons of religious tradition — inclined to combine Greek elements with traditional Oriental features. The situation occupied by these peoples on the border between the Roman and Parthian empires influenced them in both directions. The results of this ambivalence are evident in their figurative and decorative art.

Greek Influences

The earliest evidence of the influence of Greek art in the East — though of an indirect kind, coming via Cyprus — is provided by the remains of votive offerings found in sanctuaries at Amrit and Makmish *(Plate 73)*, north of Tel Aviv, and at Tell es-Safi in the Judaean hills. These are mainly terracotta statuettes, ranging from the " Persian horseman " and Oriental fertility goddesses to figures of athletes in archaic Greek style, which survived in Cyprus into the classical period of Greece proper.

These are, however, probably imported. Better evidence for the gradual penetration into Phoenicia of the Greek style of representing human features and garments can be found in the Umm el-Awamid stelae *(Plate 72)*, particularly in the relief of a woman praying.

At El-Kharayib considerable numbers of statuettes were found, ranging from Oriental to purely Hellenistic types. Here too a series of developing types can be identified, leading from the stiff and stylised garments of Oriental art, with their parallel folds, to the natural and free-flowing style of the Greeks.

A third class of object in which we can trace a similar process consists of the anthropoid coffins of Sidon. In the earliest examples of this type the lid bears a head obviously modelled on the Egyptian mummies and following the stylistic conventions of Egypt. As time goes on these Egyptian conventions gradually disappear, and the coffins conform with the Greek canons for the representation of the features and with Greek methods of representing the hair — developing from a stylised arrangement of blobs representing curls to a free-flowing and naturalistic hair style.

Both Syria and Palestine were inhabited for long periods by peoples with a strong prejudice against the representation of the human form in the round, and their iconoclastic tendencies were naturally directed first and foremost against works of classical sculpture, which were attacked and mutilated by Jewish, Christian and Moslem zealots. It is not surprising, therefore, that so few examples of this sculpture survive, and those few in a sadly mutilated condition. Enough is left, however, to make it possible to say with assurance that all the many different trends in 4th century Greek art are represented in Syria and Palestine, though in many cases only in comparatively late Roman copies.

The athletic school of Polycleitus is perhaps the one least suited to the Oriental taste ; but even so there are a few examples of this square and solid type of male figure, like the statue of a youth *(Plate 74)* found in the theatre at Beth-Shean (Scythopolis).

It is evident that the Hellenistic East, with its strong monarchic rule and its deification of kings during their life, offered wide scope for the Lysippean school of portraiture. One of the earliest examples of this influence is the so-called "Alexander Sarcophagus" *(Plates 76, 77)*, the finest but not the only example of its kind found in the royal necropolis of Sidon. This is in all probability the coffin of King Abdonymus of Sidon, who was restored to the throne of his ancestors by Alexander and may accordingly have been led to commission his coffin from a Greek artist. The carvings on the sides of the sarcophagus symbolise the hoped-for union of Greeks and Orientals under the rule of the Macedonian conqueror. On one side is a battle between Greeks and Persians *(Plate 76)*, showing Alexander in the forefront of the fighting ; on the other is a hunting scene *(Plate 77)* in which Greeks and Orientals act together. The likeness of Alexander on the coffin is a reproduction of the Lysippean type. While the main scenes have the free-flowing multi-coloured character of Hellenistic reliefs the vine tendrils round the lid show a stylised angular pattern which looks like an early example of the Orientalising style.

Another Lysippean bust found at Beth-Shean has been interpreted as either Dionysius or Alexander. It shows clear traces of colouring in the hair, which has the two characteristic curls of divinity in front. The contrast between the smooth face and the towering hair is excellently contrived. A bust of Antiochus III, now in the Louvre, is also a masterpiece of Hellenistic portraiture, combining sharp individualisation with typological idealisation. There are also numerous portrait heads of Emperors which combine Hellenistic technique with Roman realism.

The third main school of 4th century sculpture, which had numerous ramifications in Hellenistic Asia Minor, was that of Scopas, the sculptor of *pathe* — a Greek term which comprehends both "feeling" and "suffering". The Scopaic school developed into the baroque tendencies which are evident during the Hellenistic period both at Pergamon and Rhodes. This appeal to the feelings of the spectator was not without its attractions to the emotive nature of the Oriental peoples. We find evidence of its survival in the 2nd century head of Zeus Serapis found at Gerasa *(Plate 75)*, with its expression of overpowering gravity. The wrinkled brow, uplifted glance, slightly open mouth and emaciated cheeks are full of Scopaic feeling, while the heavy flow of hair and beard emphasises the majesty of the god.

Fragments of two statues found at Philadelphia, probably Roman copies of Hellenistic originals, are reminiscent of Pergamene sculpture in the impression they convey of vigorous action and strong feeling — indeed of agony. The two figures apparently belonged to the same group ; one of them, a giant or barbarian with a violently contorted face *(Plate 78)*, seems to have been carrying a smaller figure, perhaps a child. The execution of this work is of a very high order, particularly in the anatomy of the leg and the twisted muscles of the bearded face.

As might be expected, the fourth school of 4th century Greek sculpture, that of Praxiteles, with its insistence on sensuous softness, was the one most appreciated in the East. The uppermost level of the prehistoric cave on Mount Carmel produced one example of a Praxitelean work — a standing terracotta figure of a nude Aphrodite *(Plate 83)* leaning on an Ionic column, with a periscelis round her thighs and a necklace on her breast ; she seems to have been holding a mirror or an apple in her right hand. The inscription on the back, " Paionias panchares " (" Paionias is very happy "), is early Hellenistic in character. There are numerous other copies of the standing or crouching Aphrodite — a variation devised by Daedalsos of Bithynia. The two finest are bronze statuettes now in the Louvre.

Another figure of the Praxitelean school is a statue of a dancing satyr *(Plate 82)* found at Caesarea, a smiling youth looking down at a dog crouched at his feet — a Roman copy of a 3rd century original, probably made in Alexandria. A very similar figure was found at Iol Caesarea in Africa. The Silenopappus carved from ivory which was found near the castle of Sidon, with its soft modelling and wistful glance, belongs to the same group of Dionysiac figures.

One type of statuary which originated in Hellenistic Syria and spread widely throughout the Greco-Roman world was the Tyche of Antioch, as conceived by Eutychides, a pupil of Lysippus. The goddess is represented sitting on a rock, with a youth who symbolises the river Orontes swimming at her feet ; she holds a sheaf of corn, a symbol of fertility, in her right hand, while her left rests on a rock. She is dressed in a long cloak which hangs in many folds, and on her head is a characteristic symbol — the turreted mural crown. This type of anthropomorphic symbolism, well suited to the allegorical tastes of the Hellenistic period, was imitated by countless cities, regardless whether it was appropriate to their own geographical situation or not. Among the many Tychai which have been found those of Ptolemais (with the river Belus replacing the Orontes at the goddess's feet), Dura and Palmyra may be mentioned. In the latter cases the facial type was modified to suit the Orientalising tendencies of these cities.

In addition to the images of Greek gods who had crossed the Mediterranean and become identified with Oriental deities, we find Greco-Roman representations of the gods of the East. The best known of these are Heliopolitan Zeus, Ephesian Artemis *(Plate 81)*, Jupiter Dolichenus and Mithras. Here the scope for artistic freedom was severely limited by ritual requirements. In most cases only the visible parts of the divine anatomy and the proportions of the whole correspond to the canons of Greek art : all the rest was prescribed. Thus Heliopolitan Zeus and Artemis had both to be clad in a long clinging garment which effectively concealed their figures, and the goddess had also to wear a string of breast-shaped ornaments, symbols of her fertilising power ; only in the adornment of the cloak could Greek taste express itself. Jupiter Dolichenus had to be mounted on a bull ; Mithras must be shown slaying a bull, with his cloak streaming in the wind. In all these cases the artists had to compromise between the realism of Greek art and the ritualistic requirements of the East.

Palmyrene Sculpture

The architectural ornament of the Palmyrene temples, the funeral banquets carved on the towers and hypogaea round the city and on the funerary slabs with the portraits of the dead have provided us with hundreds of examples of Palmyrene sculpture, and their number grows with every excavation. A relatively high proportion of Palmyrene sculptures are dated by inscriptions, so that we are able to follow stylistic and other developments and to analyse them in the light of a definite chronology.

The earliest reliefs found at Palmyra do not show the frontal convention typical of all later work, but represent a procession of worshippers in the normal profile view of Oriental art. From the beginning of the 1st century A.D. frontality appears to prevail, as is shown by the oldest reliefs from the Temple of Bel, in which a procession of veiled women, together with a camel carrying a tent, is shown passing a group of people standing in the upper part of the scene (i.e. in the background); the whole group is shown frontally. In the 2nd century total frontality becomes the rule. Thus in a carving or painting of a group of people involved in some common action — for example a sacrifice — the various figures are not shown turned towards one another as the action would require, but all of them — gods, sacrificers, attendants — face the spectator. An example of this total frontality is found in a relief dating from the beginning of the Christian era showing a sacrifice to the gods Hadad, Malak and Genneas, in which the gods and the attendants are all uncompromisingly frontal. The same convention is rigidly adhered to in a relief of 154 A.D. in which the sacrificer stands between two mounted gods, and in another of 198-199, with a similar theme. The convention is slightly modified in a carving of a group of figures on the tomb of Maqqai (229 A.D.), in which a timid three-quarters view is attempted. It is observed in most of the other tombs, from that of Khitot (40 A.D.) to that of Jarhai (2nd century). The composition of the Palmyrene reliefs is characterised by lack of depth, the superimposition of background figures and flatness of execution, with little sign of Greek influence. The Greek manner can perhaps be felt only in the architectural ornament, with its vigorous plant motifs. Even here, however, some tendency to stylisation appears.

Greco-Roman influences appear in Palmyrene sculpture only incidentally. An exception is perhaps to be found in the adoption of the bust as the representational type of portrait, for this was unknown in the East. Otherwise we can point only to externals, like the frequent appearance of the Greek type of cloak and the Greco-Roman cuirass. The occasional exact reproduction of the image of a Greek god, like the Hercules in an early relief found under the Temple of Bel, is exceptional.

In itself Palmyrene sculpture is very far removed from Greek. To the Greek artist even a clothed figure was a body underneath the dress, the folds of which were determined by the living form within. To the Palmyrene the linear outline of the mass was the dominant factor, and there was no attempt to give the feel of the body. This overall mass was subdivided by linear ornaments more or less corresponding to the natural positions of folds and of limbs, but not determined by them. In the faces the individual features were submerged in the typical, and the various parts of the face were produced by sharply cut and sharply defined planes. Only in the exceptional case were wrinkles shown, with the effect of enlivening the surface. The mouth is usually lacking in expression — although in the late 3rd century the worried expression of contemporary Roman portrait heads influenced Palmyrene work. The faces are symmetrical, with the two halves exactly similar ; and this alone, being contrary to nature, would be sufficient to deaden the expression. In order to lend life to funerary busts, as their symbolic significance required, the sculptors accentuated the eyes, enlarging their size, altering their shape and indicating the pupils. By these means they achieved the transcendent " spiritual " look which is the chief characteristic of these busts.

The lack of individuality in the features was apparently intended, for the busts were made either during the lifetime of the person represented or soon after his death. The pose, in particular the position of the hands, seems to have been rigidly prescribed. The men *(Plate 84)* are shown holding some object (a scroll or a handkerchief) in the left hand, while their right is clutching the folds of their robe. The women *(Plate 85)* hold their veil in one hand, as if about to draw it aside, while the other hand grasps a spindle or some other object connected with feminine pursuits. The only variations in the stereotyped scheme are dictated by changes in fashion. Thus the general adoption of the beard from the time of Hadrian onwards had its influence on Palmyrene sculpture, although this detail too was subordinated to the general linear scheme, the beard being stylised and set in sharp contrast to the smooth face.

Differences in the ability of the artist can of course be felt even through the schematic character of Palmyrene sculpture ; and some of these anonymous artists achieved masterpieces of poignant feeling, as in a female bust, dated to 161, now in Beirut.

As was usual in Oriental art, the Palmyrene sculptors combined indifference to individual characterisation with a surprising realism in the representation of accessories. The smallest details of men's dress were reproduced, including the embroideries on their tunics and trousers, and the lavish jewellery of the Palmyrene ladies was depicted with minute fidelity. The uniforms of the various military units, camel-riders, etc., were also treated in detail. Landscape, however, was non-existent.

Nabataean Sculpture

Palmyrene influence extended over a wide area. The sculpture found at Dura Europos, for example, mostly reflects the same conventions. Such Nabataean figurative representations as have come down to us, though somewhat earlier than the bulk of the Palmyrene work, are based on the same principles. This applies, indeed, to all Nabataean work. There is of course a considerable difference between the sculpture produced in the capital, Petra, and provincial work from Tannur or the Hauran. The head of Zeus Hadad found at Petra in 1954 is richly ornamented and shows some stylisation of the hair, beard and wreath, but is otherwise classical in style ; but a head of Hermes found with it has a full face and chin, snail curls and patterned whiskers of Oriental type.

The Tannur sculptures date mainly from the third phase of this temple, i.e. from the early 2nd century A.D. Some of them, like the seated Hadad, follow Greek prototypes in their facial expression and dress but betray their Oriental connections in the exaggerated proportions of the head and eyes. Some of the heads of Hadad *(Plate 79)* are purely Oriental, sacrificing verisimilitude to religious expressionism. The hair is represented by a series of parallel ridges arranged symmetrically ; the wrinkles on the brow form a linear ornament ; the eyes are encircled by raised oval outlines and have centred pupils, dominating the lower part of the face, which has a stylised moustache and a curly beard enclosing the oval outline of the face. Similar stylisations, though not always carried to such extremes, are apparent in the other male heads from Tannur.

The representations of female deities have the rounded, symmetrical faces, large eyes and stylised hair of their male counterparts. A convention peculiar to female figures is the arrangement of the folds of their dresses in such a way as to suggest a wind blowing straight in their face — a convention which goes back to the winged Victories of classical Greece but is applied here in a schematic fashion. The geometrisation of the wings of the Victories and of eagles is another Oriental feature found at Tannur.

The Nabataean tradition is also evident in the statuary from the Hauran, mainly of Roman date, collected and published by Dunand. These works are closely connected with Palmyra in style. Frontality is much in evidence even in such subjects as the Judgment of Paris (on a lintel from the ancient Canatha) in which the figures are placed side by side. In dress and accessories, however, the Nabataean statues are Hellenistic in type; Oriental mounted figures are rare.

Nabataean sculpture seems to be the expression of a settled agricultural people, with much more interest in the gods of fertility and viticulture than in those who protected the caravan trade. The vine god Dushara and Atargatis, goddess of fish and corn, are prominently represented. The evidence we have appears to date from the final stages of Nabataean history, when Roman intervention had greatly circumscribed their activities in the desert and forced them to seek a living by cultivating the soil. This corresponds to what we know of the achievements of King Rabel II, who "gave life to his people" by extending the cultivated area and constructing dams and irrigation channels in the Negeb and elsewhere. This change, brought about by the circumstances of economic life, is reflected in Nabataean art.

2. PAINTING AND THE MINOR ARTS

Painting

Owing to the fragility of the material painting is much more poorly represented in the surviving remains than the other arts. Apart from a few painted stelae of the Ptolemaic period from the Phoenician coast, the frescoes that have come down to us were almost all found in tombs. Only in the desert areas, and particularly at Dura Europos, have wall paintings been preserved to any appreciable extent.

Among the earliest examples of this art are the frescoes in the Hellenistic tombs at Marissa (Tell Sandahanna), dating from the 2nd and 1st centuries B.C. The main fresco, above the loculi in the long sides of the tomb, depicts a hunting scene, a procession of animals (including an elephant, a rhinoceros and a giraffe) and a series of mythological beasts and fishes (a bull with a bearded human face, elephant-fishes, etc.). Here we clearly have a reflection of the royal zoological garden of the Ptolemies, which included rare African animals, and also of the Greek manuals of zoology in which the theory of the parallelism of land and sea animals was propounded. The short side of the tomb has a symbolic representation of an eagle, garlands, two lighted candelabra and funerary urns. Another painting in a neighbouring tomb shows a pair of musicians ; the figures are represented in profile, using few colours, but the drawing is correct and lively.

Other tomb paintings have been found in the coastal area. A tomb of Roman date at Ascalon, with a fresco of two nymphs seated by a spring and a rich Dionysiac ceiling, seems from the Nilotic flora to have Egyptian affinities. Another painting of a man and woman with Hymen between them was found at Nahariya. Round Tyre and Sidon, and as far away as Massyaf, painted tombs have been found, usually decorated with vine trellises, birds, garlands and sometimes mythological scenes of the type common on sarcophagi. The draughtsmanship is generally free and flowing, the hellenised artists being well trained in the artistic *koine* of the period.

A fresco from Petra showing a vintage scene with Erotes corresponds to the usual Hellenistic type. Rather more interesting is a painted tomb at Marwa (Transjordan) in which Pluto and Proserpina, accompanied by Cerberus, are shown enthroned above a dado with three female masks.

The few surviving paintings in Palmyrene tombs and the many frescoes found at Dura Europos represent quite a different trend. The frescoes in the " Tomb of the Three Brothers " at Palmyra correspond to some extent with Hellenistic standards ; but even here the " spiritual " expression of Oriental art is in evidence. The frescoes at Dura revealed a whole unsuspected world of painting, which was at once hailed as an " Oriental forerunner of Byzantine painting ". The first paintings to come to light were those in the temple of Bel, followed by many others, including those in the temple of

Zeus Theos, the House of the Roman Scribes and, last but not least, the Christian church and the synagogue. Although there were many different painters working at Dura they followed the same stylistic principles. The composition is hieratic, the figures being positioned frontally on a kind of podium. The background is simplified to either a single building façade or a flat space. The size of each figure is in proportion to its importance, with the principal deities or heroes towering over the rest. The dress of the various personages is realistic : the townspeople wear a tunic and himation in the Greek fashion, the priests are dressed in their sacred robes with high conical hats, the women are sumptuously adorned in Palmyrene style, while the gods, heroes, kings and their attendants — the whole apparatus of authority in heaven and on earth — wear the Parthian costume of a short riding tunic, trousers and boots. The frontality is absolute : with very few exceptions all the figures look straight at the spectator, in whatever activity they are engaged — whether offering sacrifice, fighting, or even cutting off someone's head. The faces are depicted by a Hellenistic shorthand convention, no more than eleven strokes being needed. Stress is always laid on the eyes, which are large and have a fixed stare which adds to their "spirituality". In representing action the method of consecutive narration is adopted, the same figure appearing again and again in the successive scenes in which the story develops.

The paintings in synagogues and churches raise special problems related to the development of Jewish and Christian art, the origins of Biblical imagery and the spiritual content of Judaism which are outwith the scope of classical Syrian art and can be referred to only in passing.

Mosaics

Mosaic pavements have been better preserved than paintings, thanks to the more durable material of which they are made and to their lowly position. But mosaics were expensive, and their proliferation is a sure indication of economic well-being. This explains why Roman Syria is, along with Africa, the richest in mosaics of all the provinces of the Empire, while the disturbed province of Palestine has yielded hardly any pavements datable between the 1st century B.C. and the 3rd century A.D. The Masada pavements, laid by Herod, are interesting because of their early date, their endeavour to give the common Hellenistic type a touch of local colour and their strict avoidance of any representation of human beings or animals. But after these there is a gap until the Nilotic scenes in a Scythopolis pavement of the 3rd century A.D.

The richest collection of mosaics of the 1st century A.D. onwards has been found at Antioch. Owing to the large quantity of material and its reliable dating we can follow step by step the evolution of mosaic art from the early *emblemata* (pictures inset in the pavement) in the Hellenistic manner to the gradual enlargement of the picture to cover whole pavements, which are then subdivided. The subjects depicted include mythological scenes, apotropaic images, literary allusions (with special reference to dramatic performances), local topographical scenes which vividly illustrate the life of the city, and philosophical concepts. As conditions became increasingly difficult during the 3rd century A.D. stress was laid on such philosophical and economic concepts (represented by personifications) as " plenty ", " fertility ", " magnanimity " and the like, and on consolatory reflections on the passage of time (" Aeon ", the " Seasons "). The aristocratic character of late Roman society is well represented in the numerous hunting scenes (which are also found at Apamaea). The Antioch mosaics are well integrated into the Greco-Roman world, using the standard series of decorative elements. Oriental details, like the beribboned lion which interrupts a pavement pattern, or the phoenix with its halo, appear at a later stage.

The art of mosaic-working was not confined to the main cities, as we can see from a series of pavements found in the neighbourhood of Byblos, Beirut and Baalbek with mythological representations (the adventures of Jupiter), philosophical subjects (Calliope with the Seven Sages) and historical and religious themes (the birth of Alexander).

Evidently subjects of this kind did not commend themselves to Christians and Jews, and accordingly the earlier churches and synagogues adhered strictly to the geometric type of pavement. The ban on other subjects broke down only gradually, and the full flowering of mosaic figurative art did not come until Byzantine times.

Other Arts

As one of the richest and most highly developed provinces of the Roman Empire, Syria was a centre for the production of all the material amenities of an advanced civilisation, its arts and crafts being perhaps second only to those of Rome, and equal with those of Alexandria. Unfortunately the climate of Syria does not preserve metal and wood so well as the dry Egyptian desert, and most of the products of Syrian refinement have thus been lost. Among the few masterpieces which have survived is the Emesa helmet (1st century A.D.), which is fashioned of iron, silver and gold, the three metals being blended into a colourful whole. The face on the helmet is a portrait of the wearer. For all its stylisation it is the representation of an individual, and as such is related to the realism of Roman art rather than to the typological schema of the East.

Blown and moulded glass, which came into general use in the time of Augustus, was another specialty of the Phoenician and Palestinian coastal cities : indeed if we are to believe Pliny its manufacture was discovered in this region. At any rate the products of the local glass-makers, many of whom later moved to Rome, are of remarkable refinement and beauty.

Before concluding this account we should at least mention pottery — a product which is the commonest find in archaeological investigations but is of interest mainly to specialists. Although invaluable as a means of dating, the common pottery of the classical period is of the plain ribbed type which was manufactured almost everywhere. The imported *terra sigillata* and its Eastern imitations are not peculiar to Syria, although Antioch has been suggested as one of the centres of production of the so-called " Megarian " bowls, with relief decoration. The only type of locally made pottery which is of intrinsic interest is the Nabataean eggshell ware, which consists mainly of bowls of incredible fineness covered with monochrome decoration based on plants (palmettes, vines, pomegranates) or geometric motifs ; figures are extremely rare. This ware, apparently derived from late Hellenistic types, was common in Nabataean territory in the 1st century B.C. and the 1st century A.D.

CONCLUSION

OUTSTANDING PROBLEMS

The difference between periods in which our knowledge of the past is derived wholly or mainly from archaeological research and those in which we rely on written sources is reflected in the problems awaiting solution. In the former case the very foundations of historical chronology can be revolutionised by the results of an archaeological excavation, or the decipherment of an unknown script can upset old and well established basic conceptions. In the classical and post-classical periods we cannot expect such revolutions. The main outlines of events are fairly well known, and archaeological finds can merely confirm or negative doubtful points and fill in certain gaps in our knowledge. Not surprisingly, therefore, the outstanding problems in the field of classical archaeology in Syria and Palestine relate to particular matters like cultural transitions, architectural problems, questions of religious life and trends in art.

We have, for instance, comparatively little information about the penetration of Greek influences into the Near East in the pre-Hellenistic and early Hellenistic periods, and the Persian period is still largely an archaeological riddle. Occasional finds of Greek pottery or coins indicate patterns of trade, and one such splendid find as the royal necropolis at Sidon can illuminate the darkness ; but this merely accentuates the shadows that remain. The existence of Greek colonies is attested by the literary sources and by occasional finds of cemeteries belonging to Greek mercenaries ; but much more information is needed on this (so far as our subject-matter is concerned) early period.

Another field where we still grope in the dark is that of the town plans and public buildings of the Phoenician towns from Akko (Ptolemais) northwards. We know the sites of the ancient cities, which in Hellenistic times served as the acropolises of the new and enlarged metropolitan centres ; and the example of Caesarea has shown how much can be learned from air photographs, in spite of later building and cultivation. The ports of

Tyre and Sidon have indeed been explored (although at a time when the techniques of modern underwater archaeology were not available), but there has been no investigation of the other harbours which dotted the Phoenician coast.

Nor have the cities on the Phoenician coast been scientifically excavated, even in part. It is true that their continued occupation has presented serious obstacles to large-scale excavation, unless at prohibitive cost. Nevertheless the cutting of trenches at carefully selected spots and the examination of the stratification revealed in the sections might throw much light on the development of these ancient and famous cities.

The whole problem of religious life as reflected in the archaeological remains is still largely obscure. We know the names and likenesses of the principal deities and their connections with the old Semitic pantheon, but the relations between the various divinities are much less clear. Thus we still have no certain knowledge of the gods to whom the two smaller temples at Baalbek were dedicated ; nor do we know the third divinity (if there was one) of the Heliopolitan cult. The relations between Atargatis and her consort Hadad changed in the course of time, the goddess gradually gaining the superior position and reducing the status of the male deity, certainly at Hierapolis (Mabug) and possibly also at Dura : more light on this point from other sites would be welcome. The religious symbolism of the Syrian-Palmyrene gods is also still to a large extent obscure.

RELATIONS WITH PARTHIAN ART

One of the fundamental problems of Syrian archaeology is the relationship between the art of Palmyra and Dura on the one hand and Parthian art on the other. The question cannot be clarified within Syria itself ; for one of the difficulties is the absence of any evidence on Parthian art earlier than its supposed derivative at Palmyra. That city has yielded reliefs and statues dating from before the Christian era ; but there is no earlier Parthian material, and the filiation of Palmyra to Parthia thus rests merely upon a hypothesis. The monuments at Nemrut Dağ do indeed antedate the Palmyrene evidence, but here again the relationship between the art of Commagene and that of Parthia is problematical.

The question of frontality in art is closely bound up with this problem. Although there is general agreement that frontality dominated Oriental art from the 1st century onwards, the origins of this phenomenon are very much in dispute. Some scholars — with no good reason, in the present author's opinion — seek to connect it with Greek art. They assume that the traditional preference for a profile representation was abandoned under the influence of the freedom displayed in the works of Greek art which found their way to the East during the Hellenistic period. In these works the Oriental artists saw how every conceivable position (profile, three-quarters view, frontal view, etc.) could be used with great effect ; and with their traditional preference for a single aspect — so the argument goes — they selected the frontal view and thereafter adhered to it.

This simplistic view is rejected by those who look for the roots of Palmyrene and related arts in Parthian culture. There is indeed a great deal of evidence for frontality in Parthian art, but it is contemporary with the earliest evidence for this phenomenon in Palmyra, or even later. So far as our present knowledge goes, this evidence goes back to 55 at Palmyra and to 34 at Dura Europos.

A third view attributes the preference for frontality to a Syrian revival and extension of the ancient religious conception of saviour gods, who had from time immemorial been represented facing (i.e. noticing and helping) their worshippers. By a gradual extension of the idea of mystical union of both dead and living men with the god, and of the concept of saviour deities itself, the frontal position penetrated Orientalising art to the exclusion of all other attitudes. Although this third view seems the most acceptable of the three, much further research is needed to clarify the problem.

DATING OF THE MONUMENTS AT PETRA

The origins, and still more the dating, of the Nabataean monuments at Petra present another unsolved problem, owing to the paucity of dated monuments at this site. The controversy between those who assign these monuments to the Hellenistic period and those who believe them to be of Roman date has been going on for many years. On the one hand it is argued that the formal elements of Nabataean art are undoubtedly derived from the Hellenistic world, and that the Philhellene Nabataean kings preceded the period of Roman suzerainty. On the other hand the similarity between the Nabataean rock-cut façades and the stage walls of Roman theatres is stressed. Attempts to arrange the façades at Petra in a chronological series by methods of sequence dating have not been conclusive. The excavations which are now going on sporadically have indeed provided firm evidence for the later date of some of the structures, like the triumphal arch or gate. As regards some of the best known of these structures, like the temple called the Qasr Bint Farun (perhaps the temple of Aphrodite which is known from the written sources to have existed at Petra), the dating by excavators has oscillated between the Augustan and the Antonine period. Here too there is a need for thoroughgoing research both in the field and on a comparative basis.

The fact is that most of the remains of the classical period can be dated without recourse to that standby of the archaeologist in earlier levels, the pottery ; and this has led to a comparative neglect of this type of evidence, a neglect which has had certain unfortunate effects on archaeological research. While intensive investigations and comparative studies have reduced the uncertainty in dating Iron or Bronze Age pottery to within a hundred or even fifty years, the margin in dating common pottery of later periods is often two or three centuries. It is thus one of the most important tasks of the present-day archaeologist to establish a reliable sequence of pottery types. Excavations like those at Masada, where the finds can often be pinpointed to a particular year, may be expected to provide us with fixed points of reference ; and, starting from these, the rest of the field can be surveyed and charted out.

ORIGINS AND DEVELOPMENT OF JEWISH ART

Problems peculiar to Palestine arise in relation to Jewish art. There are two main difficulties in this field. First, we observe during the Second Temple period an intense abhorrence for all kinds of figurative art. To the surprise of the excavators it was found that even in his remote desert fastness of Masada Herod had avoided all shapes or forms representing human beings or animals ; and the same aniconic tendency is evident in the Jewish tombs round the capital and is attested in the written sources. Josephus even accounted it a sin for Solomon to have fashioned the forms of animals in his Temple, although the Bible expressly authorised this. The zoomorphic ornaments in the palace of Herod Antipas in Tiberias were roundly condemned as being against the Law, and were destroyed when the opportunity presented itself. This attitude persisted until the time of Bar-Kokhba's revolt (132-135) ; and when his soldiers captured booty from the Romans in the shape of metal bowls with handles ending in human faces they slashed the offending objects with their knives.

Yet within a century carvings of angels, men and animals began to appear in the Galilean synagogues ; sometimes even mythological subjects were permitted. The same change of attitude can be observed in the Beth-Shearim catacombs, where the patriarch Judah I (died c. 219), the great leader of Judaism, was buried. Members of his family and other sanctified rabbis were also laid to rest near his tomb, and they were followed by Jews from Phoenicia, Palmyra and even from as far afield as northern Arabia, all of whom wished to be buried near the sacred tombs. And yet not only were Greco-Roman sarcophagi with mythological representations freely re-used in these burials, but locally made coffins reproduced the once forbidden images of human beings and animals (the Roman eagle, lions devouring their prey, etc.). This complete change of attitude on the part of rabbinic Judaism requires elucidation.

In a more general sense the origins of the Jewish art of the Second Temple period are still problematical. The decoration of some of its products, like the better class tombs or sarcophagi, seems reminiscent of Palmyrene art, while for the simpler types of burial, in particular the ossuaries with their carved geometric ornament, the closest parallel is to be found in the stucco ornament of the contemporary Parthian palaces. Whether there exists a connecting link or a common ancestor of these unusual forms of ornament is another question that calls for further investigation.

Finally there remains the problem of the artistic *koine* of the period, on which the work of artists and craftsmen of all creeds was based. This problem is well exemplified by the decoration of the lead coffins which were probably made in the Phoenician cities and spread into northern and central Palestine. Since the elements in the ornamentation of these coffins were made in moulds which could be applied in any context, they were extensively used and re-used. Surprising evidence of this is provided by coffins found at Sidon and Beth-Shearim *(Plate 80)* which are identical in their ornament except that one has Christian figurative decoration while the other shows the religious symbols of Judaism. Clearly further research is required into the common tradition on which such decorative parallels were based ; but in the meantime much can be learned by considering their similarities and their local or chronological divergences.

CHRONOLOGICAL TABLE

B.C.	Syria	Palestine	Arabia	B.C.
ca. 450	Herodotus travels in Syria and Palestine			ca. 450
450-350	Greek merchants and mercenaries found settlements			450-350
332	Conquest by Alexander the Great			332
323	Death of Alexander. Ptolemy in Egypt			323
312			Demetrius Poliorcetes fails to take Petra	312
301	Seleucid rule established	Ptolemaic rule established		301
280-241	Syrian Wars between Seleucids and Ptolemies			280-241
223	Accession of Antiochus III			223
198		Antiochus III conquers Palestine		198
188	Romans defeat Antiochus III at Magnesia			188
175-163	Antiochus IV			175-163
169			Aretas I	169
167		Maccabaean revolt		167
162	Civil war in Syria begins			162
141		Judaea independent under Hasmonaeans		141
139-129	Antiochus VII Sidetes			139-129
120- 96			Aretas II (Erotimus)	120- 96
104- 76		Alexander Jannaeus		104- 76
87- 62			Aretas III Philhellen	87- 62
85	Parthians take Dura Europos Damascus occupied by Nabataean king (Aretas III)			85
64	Syria a Roman province	Judaea tributary to Rome	Nabataeans tributary to Rome	64
53	Crassus defeated by Parthians- Euphrates frontier established			53
37-4		Herod the Great		37-4
30		Fortifies Masada		30
25		Sebaste founded		25
19		Begins rebuilding of Temple		19
15	Berytus a Roman colony			15
12		Caesarea founded		12

A.D.	Syria	Palestine	Arabia	A.D.
9 B.C.-40			Aretas IV	9 B.C.-40
6		Judaea a Roman province		6
66-70		First Jewish revolt		66-70
70		Fall of Jerusalem		70
73		Fall of Masada		73
88	Palmyra : tomb-tower of Iamblichus			88
100-150	First Palmyrene style			100-150
106			Provincia Arabia set up	106
108	Palmyra : tomb of Jarhai			108
110	Town plan of Palmyra			110
111-116			Via Nova constructed	111-116
113	Palmyra : tower of Elahbel			113
117	Antioch ruined by earthquake			117
c. 130			Capital transferred from Petra to Bostra ; flourishing period of Gerasa and Philadelphia and other caravan cities.	C. 130
132-135		Second Jewish revolt (War of Bar-Kokhba)		132-135
135		Colonia Aelia Capitolina established in Jerusalem		135
140		Re-establishment of Sanhedrin		140
150-200	Second Palmyrene style			150-200
160	Tomb of Three Brothers begun at Palmyra			160
164	Romans take Dura			164
200-272	Third Palmyrene style			200-272
219		Judah I the Patriarch buried at Beth-Shearim		219
217-225	Syrian emperors			217-225
244-249	Philip the Arab (founds Philippopolis)			244-249
245	Synagogue at Dura rebuilt			245
256	Dura destroyed by Parthians			256
260	The Emperor Valerian taken prisoner			260
260-272	Palmyrene rule (under Odenath, then Zenobia)			260-272
272	Aurelian destroys Palmyra			272
284-305	Diocletian			284-305
324	Constantine the Great defeats Licinius. End of Roman period			324

BIBLIOGRAPHY

Part I

General

Y. AHARONI, *The Land of the Bible,* Philadelphia, 1962.
W.F. ALBRIGHT, *The Archaeology of Palestine,* Penguin Books, 1960.
RUTH AMIRAN, *Ancient Pottery of the Holy Land,* Brunswick, 1970.
E. ANATI, *Palestine before the Hebrews,* London, 1963.
H. BOSSERT, *Altsyrien,* Tübingen, 1951.
H. FRANKFORT, *The Art and Architecture of the Ancient Orient,* 4th rev. ed., Penguin Books, 1970.
K.M. KENYON, *Archaeology in the Holy Land,* London, 1960.
A. MALAMAT and O. EISSFELDT, "Syrien-Palästina in der zweiten Hälfte des 2. Jahrtausends bis zum Ausgang des 6. Jahrhunderts v. Chr. ", *Fischer Weltgeschichte,* II, pp. 177-221 ; III, pp. 135-203.
M. NOTH, *Geschichte Israels,* 5th ed., Göttingen, 1963.
J. PRITCHARD, *Archaeology and the Old Testament,* Princeton, 1962.
G.E. WRIGHT, *Biblical Archaeology,* Philadelphia, 1962.

Middle Bronze Age I

RUTH AMIRAN, "The Pottery of the Middle Bronze Age I in Palestine ", *Israel Exploration Journal,* 10, 1960, pp. 204-225.
W. DEVER, "The 'Middle Bronze I' Period in Syria and Palestine ", *Near Eastern Archaeology in the 20th Century,* New York, 1970, pp. 132-163.
M. KOCHAVI, *The Settlement of the Negev in the Middle Bronze Age I* (in Hebrew), Jerusalem, 1967.
P. LAPP, *The Dhahr Mirzbaneh Tombs,* Jerusalem, 1966.

Middle Bronze Age II

RUTH AMIRAN, "Tell el Yahudiyeh Ware in Syria ", *Israel Exploration Journal,* 7, 1957, pp. 93-97.
I. DUNAYEVSKY and A. KEMPINSKI, "The Megiddo Temples ", *Zeitschrift des Deutschen Palästina-Vereins,* 89, 1973, pp. 161-187.
A. KEMPINSKI, *Cana'an (Syria-Palestine) during the Last Stage of the Middle Bronze Age IIB (1650-1550 B.C.)* (in Hebrew), Jerusalem, 1974.

191

K.M. KENYON, "The Middle and Late Bronze Age Strata at Megiddo", *Levant,* I, 1969, pp. 25-60.

H. OTTO, "Die Keramik der mittleren Bronzezeit in Palästina" *Zeitschrift des Deutschen Palästina-Vereins,* 61, 1938, pp. 147-277.

OLGA TUFNELL, "The Courtyard Cemetery of Tell el Ajjul", *Bulletin of the Institute of Archaeology,* 3, 1962, pp. 1-46.

J. VAN SETERS, *The Hyksos : a New Investigation,* Yale, 1966.

Y. YADIN, "Hyksos Fortifications and the Battering-Ram", *Bulletin of the American School of Oriental Research,* 137, 1955, pp. 23-32.

Late Bronze Age

RUTH AMIRAN, "The Pottery from a Late Bronze Age Tomb in Jerusalem", *Eretz Israel,* VI, pp. 25-40.

CLAIRE EPSTEIN, *Palestinian Bichrome Ware,* Leyden, 1966.

W.A. HEURTLEY, "A Palestinian Vase Painter of the Sixteenth Century B.C.", *Quarterly of the Department of Antiquities in Palestine,* 1938, pp. 21-34.

HELENE KANTOR, "The Aegean and the Orient in the Second Millennium B.C.", *American Journal of Archaeology,* 51, 1947, pp.

F.H. STUBBINGS, *Mycenean Pottery from the Levant,* Cambridge, 1951.

OLGA TUFNELL et AL., *Lachish II, The Fosse Temple,* London, 1940.

Iron Age I

Y. AHARONI, *The Settlement of the Israelite Tribes in Upper Galilee* (in Hebrew), Jerusalem, 1957.

TRUDE DOTHAN, *The Philistines and their Material Culture* (in Hebrew, with English summary), Jerusalem, 1967.

W.A. HEURTLEY, "The Relations between 'Philistine' and Mycenean Pottery", *Quarterly of the Department of Antiquities in Palestine,* 1936, pp. 90-110.

P. LAPP, "The Conquest of Palestine in the Light of Archaeology", *Concordia Theological Monthly,* 38, 1967, pp. 287-298.

D. USSISHKIN, "Observations on some Monuments from Carchemish", *Journal of Near Eastern Studies,* 26, 1967, pp. 87-95.

Iron Age II and the Persian Period

Y. AHARONI and RUTH AMIRAN, " A New Scheme for the Sub-Division of the Iron Age in Palestine ", *Israel Exploration Journal*, 8, 1958, pp. 115-184.

E. AKURGAL, *Späthethitische Bildkunst*, Ankara, 1949.

W.F. ALBRIGHT, « Was the Age of Solomon without Monumental Art ? », *Eretz Israel*, V, 1958, pp. 1*-9*.

T. BUSINK, *Der Tempel von Jerusalem*, Leyden, 1970.

W. ORTHMANN, *Untersuchungen zur späthethitischen Kunst*, Bonn, 1971.

Y. SHILOH, " The Four-Room House, its Situation and Function in the Israelite City ", *Israel Exploration Journal*, 20, 1970, pp. 180-190.

E. STERN, *The Material Culture of the Land of the Bible in the Persian Period* (in Hebrew), Jerusalem, 1973.

D. USSISHKIN, " King Solomon's Palaces ", *Biblical Archaeologist*, 36, 1973, pp. 78-103.

Y. YADIN, " Solomon's City Wall and the Gate of Gezer ", *Israel Exploration Journal*, 16, 1966, pp. 174-186.

The Principal Sites

Ajjul, Tell el- — F. PETRIE, *Ancient Gaza*, I-V, London, 1931-52.

Alalakh — L. WOOLLEY, *Alalakh, Tell Atchana*, London, 1955.

Beersheba — Y. AHARONI et AL., *Beer-Sheba*, I, Tel Aviv, 1974.

Beit Mirsim, Tell — W.F. ALBRIGHT, *Tell Beit Mirsim*, I-III, Jerusalem, 1932-43.

Beth-Shan — A. ROWE and G. FITZGERALD, *Beth-Shan*, I-IV, Philadelphia, 1930-31.

Byblos — M. DUNAND, *Fouilles de Byblos*, I-II, Paris, 1937-58 (5 vols.).

Carchemish — D.G. HOGARTH and L. WOOLLEY, *Carchemish*, I-III, London, 1914-53.

Fara, Tell el- - F. PETRIE, *Beth Pelet*, I-II, London, 1930-32.

Gezer — R.A.S. Macalister, *The Excavations of Gezer*, I-III, London, 1912 ; W. DEVER et AL., *Gezer*, I, Jérusalem, 1970 ; II Jerusalem, 1974.

Hama — H. INGHOLT, *Rapport préliminaire sur sept campagnes de fouilles à Hama en Syrie*, Copenhagen, 1940.

Hazor — Y. YADIN et AL., *Hazor,* I-IV, Jerusalem, 1958-61 ; Y. YADIN, *Hazor* (Schweich Lectures, 1970), Oxford, 1972.

Hesi, Tell el- — F. PETRIE, *Tell el-Hesy,* London, 1891 ; F.J. BLISS, *A Mound of Many Cities,* London, 1894.

Jericho — J. GARSTANG, *The Story of Jericho,* London, 1948 ; K.M. KENYON, *Excavations at Jericho,* I-II, London, 1960-66.

Jerusalem — F.J. BLISS and A.C. DICKIE, *Excavations at Jerusalem 1894-1897 ; H. VINCENT, Jérusalem sous terre,* London, 1911 ; R. WEILL, *La Cité de David,* I-II, Paris, 1920 and 1947 ; J. SIMONS, *Jerusalem in the Old Testament,* Leyden, 1952 ; K.M. KENYON, *Jerusalem,* London, 1967.

Lachish (Tell ed-Duweir) — OLGA TUFNELL et AL., *Lachish,* I-IV, London, 1938-57.

Mardikh, Tell — A. DAVICO and G. CASTELLINO, *Missione archeologica italiana in Siria, Rapporto preliminare della campagna 1965-66,* I-II.

Megiddo — R.S. LAMON and G.M. SHIPTON and G. LOUD, *Megiddo,* I-II, Chicago, 1939-48 ; R.S. LAMON, *The Megiddo Water System,* Chicago, 1935 ; P.L.O. GUY and R.M. ENGBERG, *Megiddo Tombs,* Chicago, 1938 ; G. LOUD, *The Megiddo Ivories,* 1939.

Qatna — du Mesnil du Buisson, *Le site archéologique de Mishrifé-Qatna,* Paris, 1935.

Salahiyeh, Tell es- — H.H. VON DER OSTEN, *Die Grabungen von Tell es Salahiyeh,* Lund, 1956.

Samaria — G.A. REISNER et AL., *Harvard Excavations at Samaria,* Cambridge, Mass., 1924 ; J.W. Crowfoot, K.M. KENYON et AL., *Samaria-Sebaste,* I-III, London, 1938-57.

Ugarit (Ras Shamra) — C. SCHAEFFER et AL., *Ugaritica,* I-VI, Paris, 1939-69.

Tayinat, Tell — R. HAINES, *Excavations in the Plain of Antioch,* II, Chicago, 1971.

Zincirli — C. HUMANN and R. KOLDEWEY, *Ausgrabungen in Sendschirli,* I-V, Berlin, 1893-1943.

Part II

General

L.F. ABEL, *Géographie de la Palestine*, I-II, Paris, 1933-38.
Histoire de la Palestine depuis Alexandre le Grand jusqu'à l'invasion arabe, I-II, Paris, 1952.

M. AVI-YONAH, *Map of Roman Palestine*, Oxford, 1940.
Geschichte der Juden im Zeitalter des Talmuds, Berlin, 1962.
The Jews of Palestine : A Political History from the Bar Kokhba War to the Arab Conquest, Oxford, 1976.
The Holy Land, from the Persian to the Arab Conquest. A Historical Geography, 2nd revised ed., Grand Rapids, 1977.

E.R. BEVAN, *The House of Seleucus*, London, 1902.

H.T. BOSSERT, *Altsyrien*, Tübingen, 1951.

A. BOUCHÉ-LECLERCQ, *Histoire des Séleucides*, I-II, Paris, 1913-14.

E.S. BOUCHIER, *Syria as a Roman Province*, Oxford, 1916.

J. DOBIÁS, *Histoire de la province romaine de Syrie*, Prague, 1924.

R. DUSSAUD, *Topographie historique de la Syrie antique et médiévale*, Paris, 1927.

R. DUSSAUD, P. DESCHAMPS and H. SEYRIG, *La Syrie antique et médiévale illustrée*, Paris, 1931.

F.M. HEICHELHEIM, " Roman Syria ", in T. FRANK, *An Economic Survey of Ancient Rome*, Vol. IV, Baltimore, 1938, pp. 121-257.

A.H.M. JONES, *The Cities of the Eastern Roman Provinces*, 2nd ed. rev., Oxford, 1971.

W.O.E. OESTERLEY, *A History of Israel*, II, Oxford, 1932.

E. SCHÜRER, *Geschichte des jüdischen Volkes im Zeitalter Jesu Christi*, I-III, 4th ed., Leipzig, 1901-09 (Engl. trsl. : *A History of the Jewish People in the Time of Jesus Christ*, 5 vols, Edinburgh, 1890-93).

H. SEYRIG, " Antiquités syriennes ", 1931-, *Syria,* XII-, *passim.*

K. WATZINGER, *Denkmäler Palästinas,* II, Leipzig, 1935.

Exploration

R.E. BRÜNNOW and A. von DOMASZEWSKI, *Die Provincia Arabia,* I-III, Strasbourg 1904-09.

H.C. BUTLER, *American Archaeological Expedition to Syria,* II, New York, 1903.
Syria. Princeton Expedition, Division II, Leyden, 1919-20.

C.G. CONDER and H.H. KITCHENER, *Survey of Western Palestine,* I-III, London, 1881-1883.

N. GLUECK, " Exploration of Eastern Palestine ", I-IV, *Annual of the American Schools of Oriental Research,* XIV, XV, XVIII-XIX, XXV-XXVIII, 1934-51.

C. HUMANN and O. PUCHSTEIN, *Reisen in Kleinasien und Nordsyrien,* Berlin, 1890.

A. JAUSSEN and R. SAVIGNAC, *Mission archéologique en Arabie,* I-III, Paris, 1909-1922.

C.L. WOOLLEY and T.E. LAWRENCE, " The Wilderness of Zin ", *Palestine Exploration Fund Annual,* III, 1914.

A. MUSIL, *Arabia Petraea,* I-III, Vienna, 1907-08.

A. POIDEBARD, *La trace de Rome dans le désert de Syrie,* Paris, 1934.

E. RENAN, *Mission de Phénicie,* I-III, Paris, 1874.

D. SCHLUMBERGER, *La Palmyrène du Nord-Ouest,* Paris, 1951.

G. TCHALENKO, *Villages antiques de la Syrie du Nord,* I-III, Paris, 1953-58.

W.J. Van LIERE, " Ager centuriatus of the Roman Colonia of Emesa (Homs) ", *Annales archéologiques de la Syrie,* VIII-IX, 1958-59, pp. 55-58.

C.J.M. de VOGÜÉ, *Syrie centrale,* 1-2, Paris, 1865-77.

Excavations

Amrit (Marathus)

M. DUNAND, *Bull. Mus. Beyrouth,* VII, 1944-1945, pp. 99-107 ; VIII, 1946/8, pp. 81-107.

Antioch

Antioch on the Orontes, Princeton University, I-V, Princeton, 1934-72.

G. DOWNEY, *History of Antioch,* Princeton, 1961.

Baalbek

R. WOOD, *The Ruins of Balbec,* London, 1757.

T. WIEGAND, *Baalbek, Ergebnisse der Ausgrabungen u. Untersuchungen 1898-1905,* I-III, Berlin, 1921-25.

A. PARROT *Syria,* X, 1929, pp. 103-125.

P. COUPEL, *Syria,* XVII, 1936, pp. 321-334.

C. PICARD, *Mélanges Syriens,* I, Paris, 1939, pp. 319-343.

F. COLLART and P. COUPEL, *L'autel monumental de Baalbek,* Paris-Beyrouth, 1951 (Bibl. Instit. Franç. de Beyrouth, LII).

Beirut

J. LAUFFRAY, *Bull. Mus. Beyrouth,* VII, 1944-45, pp. 13-80 ; VIII, 1945-48, pp. 7-16.

Beth-Shearim

B. MAZAR(-MAISLER), *Beth She'arim,* I, Jerusalem, 1973.

N. AVIGAD, *Beth She'arim,* III, Jerusalem, 1976.

Byblos

J. LAUFFRAY, *Bull. Mus. Beyrouth,* IV, 1940, pp. 7-36.

Caesarea

A. FROVA et al., *Scavi di Caesarea Maritima,* Milan, 1965.

M. AVI-YONAH, *Bulletin Rabinowitz,* III, 1960, pp. 44-48.
" The Caesarea Inscription of the Twenty-Four Priestly Courses ", *The Teacher's Yoke, Trentham Memorial Volume,* Waco, Texas, 1964, pp. 46-57.

Damascus

T. WATZINGER and K. WULZINGER, *Damascus, die antike Stadt,* Berlin-Leipzig, 1921.

R. DUSSAUD, *Syria,* III, 1922, pp. 219-250.

J. SAUVAGET, *Syria,* XXVI, 1949, pp. 314-358.

Dura-Europos

F. CUMONT, *Fouilles de Doura Europos,* Paris, 1926.
Excavations at Dura Europos, Preliminary Report, I-IX, 1928-52.

C.H. KRAELING, *The Synagogue,* New Haven, 1956.
The Christian Building, New Haven, 1967.

Gerasa

C.H. KRAELING (ed.), *Gerasa,* New Haven, 1938.

Iraq el-Amir

P.W. LAPP, *Bull. Amer. Sch. Or. Res.,* 165, 1962, pp. 16-34 ; 171, 1963, pp. 8-39.

Jericho

J.L. KELSO and D.C. BARAMKI, *Ann. Amer. Sch. Or. Res.*, XXIX/XXX, 1955.

J.B. PRITCHARD, *ibid.*, XXXII/XXXIII, 1958.

Jerusalem

H. VINCENT and F.M. ABEL, *Jérusalem nouvelle*, I-IV, Paris, 1914-26.

J.J. SIMONS, *Jerusalem of the Old Testament*, Leyden, 1952.

L.H. VINCENT and M.A. STEVE, *Jérusalem de l'Ancien Testament*, I-II, Paris, 1954-56.

M. AVI-YONAH (ed.), *The Book of Jerusalem* (in Hebrew), Jerusalem, 1956.

K.M. KENYON, *Palestine Exploration Quarterly*, 1966, pp. 81 ff. *Jerusalem, Excavating 3000 Years of History*, London, 1967.

Kharayib

M. CHÉHAB, *Bull. Mus. Beyrouth*, X-XI, 1952-54.

Marissa

F.J. BLISS and R.A.S. MACALISTER, *Excavations in Palestine during the years 1898-1900*, London, 1902, pp. 52-61.

H. THIERSCH and J. PETERS, *The Painted Tombs in the Necropolis of Marissa*, London, 1905.

Masada

Y. YADIN, *Masada, Herod's Fortress and the Zealots' Last Stand.* London, 1966.

Palmyra

R. WOOD, *The Ruins of Palmyra, otherwise Tedmor in the Desert,* London, 1753.

T. WIEGAND, *Palmyra, Ergebnisse der Expeditionen von 1902 u. 1917,* Berlin-Leipzig, 1932.

A. GABRIEL, *Syria,* VII, 1926, pp. 71-92.

R. AMY, *Syria,* XIV, 1933, pp. 396-411.

A.v. GERKAN, *Berytus,* II, 1935, pp. 25-33.

H. INGHOLT, *ibid.,* pp. 58-120.

D. SCHLUMBERGER, *ibid.,* pp. 149-167.

R. AMY and H. SEYRIG, *Syria,* XVII, 1936, pp. 229-266.

H. SEYRIG, *Syria,* XVIII, 1937, pp. 1-53 ; 369-378.

K. MICHALOWSKI, *Palmyre. Fouilles polonaises 1959-1964,* I-VI, Warsaw, 1960-73.

Petra

G. DALMAN, *Petra u. seine Felsheiligtümer,* Leipzig, 1908. *Neue Petra Forschungen,* Leipzig, 1912.

W. BACHMANN, C. WATZINGER and T. WIEGAND, *Petra,* Berlin-Leipzig, 1921.

A. KENNEDY, *Petra, its History and Monuments,* London, 1925.

V.A. KAMMERER, *Pétra et la Nabatène,* Paris, 1929.

M.A. MURRAY and J.C. ELLIS, *A Street in Petra,* London, 1940.

G. and A. HORSFIELD, *Quart. Dept. Antiq. Palest.,* VII, 1938 ; IX, 1941, pp. 105-204.

P.J. PARR, *Palest. Explor. Quarterly,* LXXXIX, 1957, pp. 5-16 ; XCII, 1960, pp. 124-135.

G.R.H. WRIGHT, *ibid.*, XCIII, 1961, pp. 124-135.
Ann. Dept. Antiq. Jordan, VI-VII, 1962, pp. 24-54.

Philippopolis

P. COUPEL and E. FRÉZOULS, *Le théâtre de Philippopolis en Arabie,* Paris, 1956.

Sebaste

G.A. REISNER, C.S. FISHER and D.G. LYON, *Harvard Excavations at Samaria, 1908-1910,* I-II, Cambridge, Mass., 1924.

J.W. CROWFOOT, E.L. SUKENIK and K.M. KENYON, *Samaria,* I-III, London, 1942-57.

Scythopolis (Beth-Shan)

A. ROWE, *Topography and History of Beth Shan,* Philadelphia, 1930.

Sidon

A. POIDEBARD and J. LAUFFRAY, *Sidon,* Beirut, 1951.

Tannur

N. GLUECK, *Deities and Dolphins, The Story of the Nabataeans,* New York, 1965 (London, 1966).

Tyre

A. POIDEBARD, *Un grand port disparu, Tyr,* Paris, 1939.

Art (general)

M. AVI-YONAH, " Oriental Elements in the Art of Palestine ", *Quart. Dept. Antiq. Palest.,* X, 1942, pp. 105-151 ; XIII, 1948, pp. 128-165 ; XIV, 1950, pp. 49-80.
Oriental Art in Roman Palestine, Rome, 1961.

R. GHIRSHMAN, *Iran, Parthians and Sassanians* (The Arts of Mankind), London, 1962.

C. HOPKINS, *Berytus*, III, 1936, pp. 1-30.

M. ROSTOVTZEFF, *Dura Europos and its Art*, Oxford, 1938.
Yale Classical Studies, V, 1935, pp. 155-193.

D. SCHLUMBERGER, *Syria*, XXXVII, 1960, pp. 131-166 ; 253-318.

L. WOOLLEY, *Mesopotamia and the Middle East* (Art of the World), London, 1961.

Architecture

R. AMY, *Syria*, XXVII, 1950, pp. 82-136.

N. AVIGAD, *Ancient Monuments in the Kidron Valley* (in Hebrew), Jerusalem, 1954.

E. FRÉZOULS, *Syria*, XXXVI, 1959, pp. 202-208 ; XXXVIII, 1960, pp. 54-85.

H. KOHL and C. WATZINGER, *Antike Synagogen in Galiläa*, Leipzig, 1916.

D. KRENCKER-ZSCHIETZMANN, *Römische Tempel in Syrien*, Berlin-Leipzig, 1938.

D. SCHLUMBERGER, *Syria*, XIV, 1933, pp. 283-317.

H. SEYRIG, *Syria*, XXI, 1940, pp. 277-337.

Sculpture

M. DUNAND, *Le musée de Soueida*, Paris, 1934.

J.H. ILIFFE, " A Heroic Statue from Philadelphia - Amman ", *D.M. Robinson Festschrift*, I, St Louis, Mo., 1951, pp. 705-712.

H. INGHOLT, *Studier over Palmyrensk Skulptur*, Copenhagen, 1928.
Berytus, I, 1934, pp. 32-43.

M. MOREHART, *Berytus,* XII, 1956/57, pp. 53-83.

H. SEYRIG, *Syria,* XV, 1934, pp. 155-186.
Berytus, III, 1936, pp. 137-140.
Syria, XXI, 1940, pp. 113-122 ; XXII, 1941, pp. 31-44.
Syria, XXVII, 1950, pp. 250-260.

D. SIMONSEN, *Sculptures et inscriptions de Palmyre,* Copenhagen, 1889.

Painting

J.H. BREASTED, *Oriental Forerunners of Byzantine Painting,* Chicago, 1924.

F. CHAPOUTHIER, *Syria,* XXXI, 1963, pp. 172-211.

DU MESNIL DU BUISSON, *Les peintures de la Synagogue de Doura Europos,* Rome, 1939.

E.R. GOODENOUGH, *Jewish Symbols in the Greco-Roman Period,* IX-XI, New York, 1964.
H. INGHOLT, *Acta Archaeologica,* III, 1932, pp. 1-20.
Berytus, II, 1935, pp. 58 ff.

Mosaics

M. AVI-YONAH, *Mosaic Pavements in Palestine,* Oxford, 1934.

M.H. CHÉHAB, *Bull. Mus. Beyrouth,* XIV-XV, 1957-59.

Israel Ancient Mosaics, UNESCO, 1960.

LIST OF ILLUSTRATIONS

12 *Ivory and bone plaques from El-Giser. First half of 18th century B.C. Rockefeller Museum, Jerusalem. Israel Department of Antiquities and Museums.*

13 *Scabbard from Byblos. Gold and bone. 20th-19th century B.C. Beirut Museum.*

14 *Painted juglet from Ginossar. Height 14 cm. End of 19th century B.C. Israel Department of Antiquities and Museums.*

15 *Figurine of a god holding a mace. Copper and gold. From Ugarit. 20th century B.C. Damascus Museum.*

16 *Gold ear-ring in the form of a falcon from Tell el-Ajjul. 17th century B.C. Rockefeller Museum, Jerusalem. Israel Department of Antiquities and Museums.*

17 *Gold objects from Tell el-Ajjul. 17th century B.C. Rockefeller Museum, Jerusalem. Israel Department of Antiquities and Museums.*

18 *Bichrome krater from Tell Nagila, showing a bull being dragged to an altar. Height 30 cm. About 1600 B.C. Israel Museum, Jerusalem. Israel Department of Antiquities and Museums.*

19 *Ritual axe in the form of a hand from Beth-Shean (stratum VII). 18 cm long. 14th century B.C. Rockefeller Museum, Jerusalem. Israel Department of Antiquities and Museums.*

20 *Canaanite plaque from Megiddo (stratum VIIA). About natural size. First half of 12th century B.C. Rockefeller Museum, Jerusalem. Israel Department of Antiquities and Museums.*

21 *Statue of King Idrimi of Alalakh. Height 110 cm. Beginning of 15th century B.C. British Museum, London.*

22 *Facade and staircase of Idrimi's palace at Alalakh (stratum IV). Beginning of 15th century B.C. Institute of Archaeology, Tel Aviv University. (Photo A. Hay).*

23 *Ivory head of a prince from Ugarit. Probably 13th century B.C. Damascus Museum.*

24 *Ceremonial axe from Ugarit. Bronze and silver with gold inlays. 14th century B.C. Damascus Museum.*

25 *Gold bowl with animal motifs from Ugarit. 14th-13th century B.C. Damascus Museum.*

26 *Bed-panel from the royal palace at Ugarit, showing a cult scene. 13th century B.C. Damascus Museum.*

27 *Gold bowl from Ugarit, showing the king as a hunter. 15th(?)-14th century B.C. Damascus Museum.*

28 *Ivory head from the Late Bronze Age temple at Lachish. Height c. 5 cm. 13th century B.C. Rockefeller Museum, Jerusalem. Israel Department of Antiquities and Museums.*

29 *Cult objects* (masevot), *altar and statues from the cella of Temple C at Hazor. 14th-13th century B.C. Hazor Expedition. Israel Museum, Jerusalem. Israel Department of Antiquities and Museums.*

30 *Philistine "beer-jug" from Tell Ayetun. 12th century B.C. Israel Department of Antiquities and Museums.*

31 *"Four-room house" from stratum 2 at Tell Masos. 12th-11th century B.C. Institute of Archaeology, Tel Aviv University. (Photo A. Hay).*

32 *Philistine krater from Tell Sippor. Height 22 cm. 12th century B.C. Israel Department of Antiquities and Museums.*

33 *Philistine rhyton in the shape of a boar or lion from Tell Qasileh. 12th century B.C. Haaretz Museum, Tel Aviv, Courtesy of A. Mazar. (Photo A. Hay).*

34 *Sarcophagus of King Ahiram of Byblos ; rear view. About 1000 B.C. Beirut Museum.*

35 Decorated pillar base from hilani entrance at Tell Tayinat. Height 70 cm. 9th century B.C. Courtesy of Archaeological Museum, Antakya. (Photo A. Hay).

36 Pillar base in the form of two lions from the entrance to the megaron-like temple at Tell Tayinat. 9th century B.C. Courtesy of Archaeological Museum, Antakya. (Photo A. Hay).

37 Hazor: air view of buildings in Israelite citadel. 9th-8th century B.C. Courtesy of Hazor Expedition.

38 Doorway with two Proto-Ionic capitals in the main citadel building at Hazor. Height 3 m (the restoration is probably too low). 9th century B.C. Hazor Expedition. Israel Museum, Jerusalem. Israel Department of Antiquities and Museums.

39 Window balustrade from Ramat Raḥel. Height 36 cm. Proto-Ionic style. 8th-7th century B.C. Israel Museum, Jerusalem. Israel Department of Antiquities and Museums.

40 Cult object (masevah) and two altars in cult chamber of Arad temple. 9th-7th century B.C. Arad Expedition. Institute of Archaeology, Tel Aviv University.

41 Air view of Tell Beersheba excavations at the end of the fifth season. Institute of Archaeology, Tel Aviv University.

42 Selected group of Phoenician pottery. 10th-8th century B.C. Israel Department of Antiquities and Museums.

43 Pottery figurine of a harpist from Ashdod. 8th century B.C. Ashdod Expedition. Israel Department of Antiquities and Museums.

44 Part of an ivory box from Samaria, in local Syro-Palestinian style. 9th century B.C. Rockefeller Museum, Jerusalem. Israel Department of Antiquities and Museums.

45 *Ivory sphinx from Samaria, in Phoenician style. 9th century B.C. Rockefeller Museum, Jerusalem. Israel Department of Antiquities and Museums.*

46 *Seal of Hamon* (hmn) *from Megiddo. 8th century B.C. Rockefeller Museum, Jerusalem. Israel Department of Antiquities and Museums.*

47 *Proto-Canaanite alphabetic inscription with the name* klb *(Kaleb ?). From Gezer. 17th-16th century B.C. Rockefeller Museum, Jerusalem. Israel Department of Antiquities and Museums.*

48 *Seal of Tobshalem* (tbslm) *from Ein-Gedi. 4.5 cm by 3.5 cm. About 600 B.C. Ein-Gedi Expedition. Israel Department of Antiquities and Museums.*

49 *Persian clay figurine of a nude woman from Tell Megadim. Height 15 cm. 5th century B.C. Megadim Expedition. Courtesy of M. Broshi. Israel Department of Antiquities and Museums.*

50 *Silver bowl and ladle of Persian period. From Tell Farah (South). Rockefeller Museum, Jerusalem. Israel Department of Antiquities and Museums.*

51 *Gerasa : Forum and colonnaded street. 1st century A.D.*

52 *Gerasa : propylaea leading to Temple of Artemis.*

53 *Baalbek : coffered ceiling (seen from below) of Temple of Bacchus.*

54 *Baalbek : Temples of Jupiter (left) and Bacchus (right).*

55 *Kefar Baram (Upper Galilee) : façade of synagogue, with three entrances. 3rd century A.D.*

56 *Baalbek : Temple of Bacchus, view through doorway into cella.*

57 *Capernaum : synagogue, interior with restored north wall and colonnade. 3rd century A.D.*

58 *Capernaum : synagogue, detail of decorated frieze (lintel). 3rd century A.D.*

59 *Masada : caldarium (hot room) of large bath-house in Roman style, showing the pillars of clay brick in hypocaust.*

60 *Masada : northern palace, south wall of lower terrace, with engaged columns and painted wall panels. Herodian.*

61 *Masada : mosaic floor in western palace. Herodian. Courtesy of Israel Exploration Society, Jerusalem.*

62 *Caesarea : high level Roman aqueduct bringing water from Mount Carmel. End of 1st century B.C. to beginning of 1st century A.D.*

63 *Jerusalem : rock-cut funerary monument on eastern slope of Kidron valley, "Tomb of Absalom". Beginning of 1st century A.D.*

64 *Jerusalem : rock-cut funerary monument on eastern slope of Kidron valley, "Tomb of Zechariah". Second half of 1st century B.C.*

65 *Caesarea : Roman theatre, with restored seating. 1st-3rd century A.D.*

66 *Jerusalem : temenos wall of Temple area (western wall). Herodian.*

67 *Petra : the Ed-Deir tomb, a Nabataean rock-cut funerary monument. Height 42 m. Late 1st to early 2nd century A.D.*

68 *Beth-Shearim : façade (partly restored) of Catacomb 20. 2nd-4th century A.D.*

69 *The Mask Sarcophagus from Catacomb 20, Beth-Shearim End of sarcophagus : garland between two columns, with the head of a bearded man above it. Stone, with carving. Height of sarcophagus 90 cm, of mask 20 cm.*

70 *The Lion Sarcophagus from Catacomb 20, Beth-Shearim. Stone, with carving of a lion (to left) and lioness about to drink from a vessel between them. Length of sarcophagus 2.48 m.*

71 *End of marble sarcophagus from Beth-Shearim : Leda and the swan. Height 87.5 cm. Second half of 2nd century A.D. Rockefeller Museum, Jerusalem. Israel Department of Antiquities and Museums.*

72 *Stele of Baalsamar, from Umm el-Awamid. Height 1.17 m. 2nd century B.C. Beirut Museum.*

73 *Terracotta figurine of Heracles from Makmish. Height 27 cm. 4th century B.C. Israel Museum, Jerusalem. Israel Department of Antiquities and Museums.*

74 *Marble statue of male deity, perhaps Apollo, from the Roman theatre at Beth-Shean. Height c. 1.80 m. Roman period. Israel Museum, Jerusalem. Israel Department of Antiquities and Museums.*

75 *Head of Zeus from Gerasa. 2nd century A.D. Amman Museum.*

76 *The Alexander Sarcophagus (cf. Plate 77) : detail from battle scene.*

77 *The Alexander Sarcophagus, found at Sidon. Marble. Length 3.18 m. Long side : hunting scene. End of 4th century B.C. Archaeological Museum, Istanbul.*

78 *Marble sculpture group of a giant and child, from Philadelphia (Amman) : provisional reconstruction. Probably a Roman copy of a Hellenistic original. Height of figure 1.90 m. Amman Museum.*

79 *Nabataean head of Hadad in Orientalising style, from Tannur. Amman Museum.*

80 *Decorated lead coffin from Beth-Shearim, with seven-branched candlestick and other Jewish symbols. Length c. 2 m. First half of 4th century A.D. Israel Museum, Jerusalem. Israel Department of Antiquities and Museums.*

81 *Marble statue of Artemis Ephesia found near the Roman theatre in Caesarea. Height c. 1.65 m. 2nd century A.D. Israel Museum, Jerusalem. Israel Department of Antiquities and Museums.*

82 *Marble statue of a satyr playing with a panther, from Caesarea. Roman copy of a Hellenistic original. Height c. 1.30 m. Israel Museum, Jerusalem. Israel Department of Antiquities and Museums.*

83 *Terracotta figurine of Aphrodite from Mount Carmel. Height 37 cm. 4th-3rd century B.C. Rockefeller Museum, Jerusalem. Israel Department of Antiquities and Museums.*

84 *Male bust from Palmyra. Height 64 cm. Ny Carlsberg Glyptotek, Copenhagen.*

85 *Limestone bust of a lady, originally brightly painted, from Palmyra. 3rd century A.D. Ny Carlsberg Glyptotek, Copenhagen.*

INDEX

Figures in italics refer to illustrations

213

220

The text and illustrations in this volume
were printed on the presses
of Nagel Publishers in Geneva

Binding by Nagel Publishers in Geneva

Legal Deposit N° 694

Printed in Switzerland

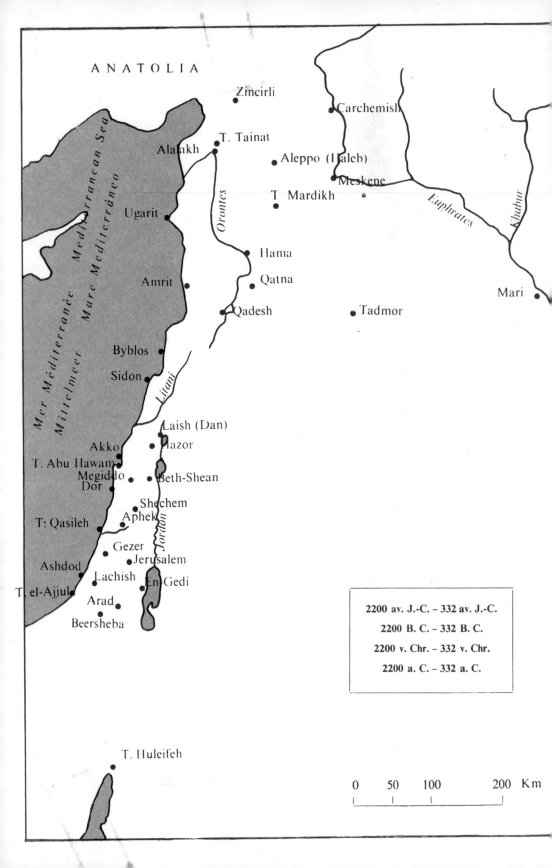

ANATOLIA

Zincirli

Carchemish

T. Tainat

Alalakh

Aleppo (Haleb)

Meskene

T. Mardikh

Orontes

Euphrates

Khabur

Mediterranean Sea

Ugarit

Hama

Mer Méditerranée *Mediterranée*
Mittelmeer *Mare Mediterráneo*

Amrit

Qatna

Mari

Qadesh

Tadmor

Mer Méditerranée
Mittelmeer

Byblos

Sidon

Litani

Laish (Dan)

Akko

Hazor

T. Abu Hawam

Megiddo

Beth-Shean

Dor

Shechem

T. Qasileh

Aphek

Jordan

Gezer

Ashdod

Jerusalem

Lachish

En Gedi

T. el-Ajjul

Arad

Beersheba

T. Huleifeh

| 2200 av. J.-C. – 332 av. J.-C. |
| 2200 B. C. – 332 B. C. |
| 2200 v. Chr. – 332 v. Chr. |
| 2200 a. C. – 332 a. C. |

0   50   100   200 Km